HOLY SMOKE

ALSO BY RICK SNEDEKER

3,001 Arabian Days

HOLY SMOKE

HOW CHRISTIANITY SMOTHERED THE AMERICAN DREAM

A BRIEF RELIGIOUS HISTORY FROM THE COLONIAL ERA TO TODAY

RICK SNEDEKER

STATION
SQUARE
MEDIA

STATION SQUARE MEDIA
NEW YORK, NEW YORK

"Holy Smoke: How Christianity Smothered The American Dream
A History of Religion From The Colonial Era To Today"

Copyright © 2020 by Rick Snedeker
Publisher: Station Square Media

Editorial Production: Janet Spencer King, www.spencerkingauthorservices.com
Cover/Interior Design: The Book Designers, www.bookdesigners.com
Production Management: Janet Spencer King, www.spencerkingauthorservices.com

Printed in the United States of American for Worldwide Distribution

ISBN: 978-1-7322395-3-1

ACKNOWLEDGEMENTS

A special thanks to Katherine Turok of whimsical-sounding Penobscot, Maine, the original editor on this previously much, much longer manuscript who, aside from kind, eloquent encouragement, provided enormously valuable advice and direction on concentrating my themes, and improving and whittling down my wordy and uneven prose.

Editor Janet Spencer King of New York City then grasped the baton and carried the project—with me in tow—across the finish line. She provided the same patient, knowledgeable, wise and endlessly good-humored guidance on *Holy Smoke* as she did on my first book, *3,001 Arabian Days*, published in 2018. In the end, we pared down a manuscript that was once 900+ pages to about 180 pages, laser-focused on the American religious experience. Assisting Janet were the group from The Book Designers who provided the cover and interior page designs, and Cristina Schreil, copy editor extraordinaire. To have such a wondrous team at hand is a *godsend* (figuratively speaking, of course).

I'd also like to acknowledge the value to this book of the many long and enjoyable discussions with my longtime best pal, Paul Sauser of Rapid City, South Dakota, about religion, philosophy, and real life, always enriched with whiskey and cigars. These chats broadened my thinking and helped place my nontheistic biases in a gentler, kinder context. Just two friends talking—one atheist, one born-again Christian—who share a veneration for dead white European philosophers, grand ideas, and human generosity. It's a recipe for endless epiphanies.

In addition, thanks go to Dr. Joe Graves, the superintendent of the Mitchell (South Dakota) Public School District, a courtly educator who explained to me the difficulties inherent in trying to insert a formal philosophy curriculum into any American school district, even though he agreed the potential benefits of learning about philosophy and critical thinking are significant and clear.

I also received excellent editorial input from Ethan Goodnight, a Harvard University Ph.D. candidate in history, who reviewed my manuscript for historical accuracy and relevance. If all the post-grads at Harvard are as astute and knowledgeable as Ethan, and as drolly funny, that iconic citadel of American scholarship is an even more special place than I had imagined.

Certainly, a nod goes to the so-called "Four Horsemen" of the "New Atheism"—elegant Richard Dawkins; the late, delightfully acerbic Christopher Hitchens; professorial Sam Harris; and avuncular Daniel Dennett. Their books educated me—as they did millions of others— about evolving understandings of atheism and clarified the dangers of institutionalized monotheistic religions on secular democracies. And at times their words made me howl with laughter.

A tip of the hat to the faceless, nameless geniuses and technologists who created the internet over many years, and innovators including Steve Jobs and Bill Gates who created the hardware and software that today empowers anonymous writers to tap that nearly infinite universe of useful knowledge with a click of a finger. They're miraculous tools.

Lastly and firstly, I appreciate the essential contributions of my wife, Pat, who reads all my stuff and always gives good, down-to-earth advice, particularly when my intent gets lost in the clouds. Her steady companionship and loving support are invaluable during the long writing, rewriting (and more rewriting), editing, and publishing process.

Thank you all.

*To historian Jennifer Michael Hecht, whose elegant, nuanced book,
"Doubt: A History," was the catalyst for this far lesser work.*

CONTENTS

PART IV: HOLDING ON | 125

PART V: MOVING ON: A PROPOSAL | 159

BLESS THE CHILDREN

AS A CHILD attending weekly Catholic catechism classes in the American Midwest more than half a century ago, my wife learned that all her non-Catholic friends were doomed to hell.

Reasonably, it terrified her.

But, it wasn't true—in doctrine or scripture or reality—even though most American Catholic kids at the time and even their parents believed the same thing, as had their Christian forebears for millennia.

Indeed, until after Pope John XXIII's revolutionary Vatican II council in 1962, when the church began to hint that non-Catholics, even non-Christians perhaps, might attain salvation, standard Catholic dogma for centuries held that heaven was barred to outliers of the faith. In fact, not until very recently did the church unambiguously revise this damning stipulation, when the last two popes—Benedict XVI in 2007,[1] and Francis I in 2013[2]—publicly assured the faithful that not only non-Catholics but even godless atheists might enter the pearly gates by personifying true goodness during their lives.

Still, for my wife, whose adult brain somewhere still harbors the assumptions of her childhood religious indoctrinations, it's in a sense too late. The damage was done long ago when the bad-seed lie of condemned children was implanted. But she still believes and retains an affection for the church and its attendant rituals and communal comforts—as do most people, even many of those who have abandoned or been sorely tested by their faiths.

So, say what you might about religion; it has impressive stamina.

Of specific importance to this manuscript is that *all* religious imaginings sown in vulnerable children's minds are entirely based on beings and realms that, as far as anyone can credibly determine, simply do not exist. Superstitions. Musings. Inventions of mind. But they are presented to kids as facts, as true, as solid threads of the material fabric of reality. Yet there's zero irrefutable verification for that. And never has been.

Nonetheless, the seeds of bad faith planted in children continue to be harvested. And the yield is bountiful.

That is the worry that spawned this book: American children are relentlessly indoctrinated with sometimes terrifying and always unverifiable Christian dogma, and the effects (e.g., religious conflict, persecution of others, private guilt, and terror) can be enduring and debilitating as they try to safely navigate the real world with their minds held hostage by potentially dangerous, unreal ideas. That cannot be a good thing. Writ large, these private Christian assumptions have morphed over history into brutal religious wars, murderous inquisitions, communal shunning and shaming of suspected naysayers, and joyless sexual repression, to name a few negative results of embedded supernatural dogma. To argue that religion has also spread and continues to spread much good in the world, which is inarguable, still does not cancel out its manifest, inevitable atrocities.

And, indoctrinating children in religious ideologies effectively perpetuates them in societies at large.

So, over several years of wide-ranging personal study, I tried to better understand the root of this phenomenon of fervent, intractable Christian faith, particularly in America. The central question I try to answer in this book is simple: Why do most Americans today continue to worship the invisible beings of Christianity when science relentlessly demonstrates that such chimeras almost certainly don't exist?

Turns out, the answer is an enigma wrapped in a riddle enfolded in a paradox. It blends the facts that the majority of early American colonists carried English Puritan values and beliefs in their mental rucksacks, that the Founding Fathers emphatically sought to separate church from the new state, and that human behavior evolving since the dawn of mankind has constantly betrayed the new nation's founding principles. This complex confusion between reality, instinct, and ideals remains.

I learned in my research that the "why" of belief, especially in America, is intensely complicated and, at the same time, crystal clear. We generally believe in chimera, it turns out, just because we simply absorb what those around us already believe, not because we have defensible reasons. Happily, a remedy exists to potentially clarify the situation, and, ironically, it would employ some of the same tools as religious indoctrination. But such an initiative would take time, and political will.

A primary obstacle to encouraging a more rational, less supernatural society is that Christian assumptions have left many if not most Americans with a biased sense that simply questioning, much less *not believing* in invisible phantasms, is irrational, likely even dangerous.

Julian Baggini, a reporter for the United Kingdom's *Financial Times*, noted in a 2012 article about Americans' continuing resistance to atheism that in interviewing unbelievers nationwide he found they often "live in isolation and secrecy," fearing disapproval of Christian believers. "In a nation that celebrates freedom of religion like no other," Baggini wrote, "freedom not to be religious at all can be as hard to exercise as the right to swim the Atlantic."[3]

Indeed, a 2016 University of Minnesota study of 2,500 adults showed that Americans then held Muslims in higher regard than atheists, despite then still-prevalent anti-Muslim sentiments stemming from the events of 9/11. The study revealed that despite atheism's six-fold growth in the US from 1972 to 2014, some 40 percent of America's godly still viewed the godless with contempt.[4]

In my research, I learned how Christianity emerged from shadow in the Middle Ages to virtually rule the Western world, with iron-fisted suppression of doubt a core element of its dogma. Martin Luther (1483–1546), the lion of the Reformation, in which Protestantism threw off Catholicism, viewed reason as "the Devil's greatest whore"[5] and intellectual curiosity as a putrid disease. The Bible was the only "truth" worth pursuing in Luther's world. The medieval Christian church disingenuously co-opted classical philosophy of the Greeks—then considered the fount of reason—to give the faith a saving patina of rationality just as Western Catholicism was being jolted by the sudden re-emergence of philosophical ideas that had lain dormant for millennia in the West after the fall of Rome. Some medieval philosophers carried on that tradition, such as French scientist Blaise Pascal, who "propagated a religious doctrine that taught the experience of God through the heart rather than through reason."[6]

This tension between faith and reason would determine how the modern world evolved with such a wide chasm—supernatural religion on one side, of which Christianity remains dominant, and science on the other, the only surviving and universally accepted fraction of reason. My goal is to encourage embracing the empirical ethos of reason when considering religion, particularly in America. That impulse has been largely dormant in the US since the so-called "Pilgrims" arrived in 1620 and the Puritans in what is now Massachusetts in 1630 and began spreading the "word of God" throughout the land.

This book attempts to explain how we Americans evolved to this dreamy, faithful state, and suggests how we might now transcend it—how we might get to a place where our children aren't routinely told that their friends will burn forever because of what their parents might believe.

"I talk to God, but the sky is empty," wrote American poet Sylvia Plath (1932–1963). In fact, this simple existential awareness of an "empty sky" is exactly how rational doubt begins.

Let's start there.

INTRODUCTION

"When even the brightest mind in our world has been trained up from childhood in a superstition of any kind, it will never be possible for that mind, in its maturity, to examine sincerely, dispassionately, and conscientiously any evidence or any circumstance which shall seem to cast a doubt upon the validity of that superstition. I doubt if I could do it myself."

—**Mark Twain** (*1835–1910*),
The Autobiography of Mark Twain

DESPITE MARK TWAIN'S insightful quote above about how indoctrinating children in superstition (i.e., religion) can permanently retard them, such a lifelong deficit is not necessarily foreordained.

Notwithstanding vigorous, prolonged religious instruction in childhood, many American kids (myself included) still retain their natural reasonableness and mature into thoughtful skeptics, agnostics, and atheists. Most, however, don't: Indeed, more than 70 percent of Americans today remain self-described Christians.[7] For true believers, Christianity is the gift that keeps on giving, over generations.

All Americans—true believers, provisional doubters, and unrepentant heathens alike—are awash in Christianity. Yet, I expect few of us ever feel even slightly damp.

When we have a day off on Sunday, that's Christianity. When the death penalty is still condoned ("an eye for an eye") or abhorred, that's Christianity. When we justify the morality of going to war ("just war"), or not, that's also Christianity. Even when we react with startled disbelief to unbelief, Christianity again. When we open a drawer in our hotel room and find the Bible there, yes, Christianity once more. Even our manners, clichés, day-to-day morality, and habits of sex and marriage, all Christianity, too. We're soaked in it.

Why? Because, a compulsion to believe in fantasies of all kinds seems deeply embedded in our genes, because the Bible has forever told us about the Christian tales, and because human nature all-too-readily accepts time-honored traditional ideas and authority. For most us, unquestioning obeisance to "received wisdom"—the cultural mythologies that we let define us—has become an indivisible part of our shared humanity.

In this country, it's just the way it is. The Christian overlay that enshrouds our society is so all-encompassing and seemingly natural, many of us probably give little thought to its many residual manifestations and effects. We aren't by law or original intent a "Christian nation," yet, in a lesser sense, we totally are. While there isn't a single formal mention of the personal Christian God or Jesus in the US Constitution or Declaration of Independence, and our founders pointedly wanted even atheists protected, somehow we've still ended up with "one nation under God" in our national Pledge of Allegiance, and "In God we Trust" on our money and on walls behind judges' benches. Countless examples clearly demonstrate how Christianity has perpetually permeated our culture, a few of which weren't stealthily stitched into public life until well into the twentieth century.

For good reasons, our Founding Fathers largely kept a personal deity out of our origin documents: They deeply feared that religious tyranny by dominant churches, a standard reality in the Europe our ancestors fled, would sabotage the American experiment. So, despite the dominance of Christianity in our embryonic nation (though few regularly attended church at the time), the founders, more Enlightenment men of reason than proponents of faith, pointedly opted to erect a foundational, if metaphorical, "wall of separation" (again, Thomas Jefferson's term) between church and state.

Political opponents of the superstition-loathing Jefferson, it's germane to point out here, painted him as un-Christian and possibly an atheist, and spread rumors he planned to ban the Bible once elected. Adding to his opponents' wariness was his flat refusal to ever publicly talk about his personal religious beliefs. In fact, Jefferson envisioned American religion as evolving into a natural spiritual practice—he called it "civic religion"—stripped of all its original supernatural elements.[8] He even compiled an annotated Bible shorn of all mysticism, devoid of all ghostly beings except an unreachably remote God who for all intents and purposes was irrelevant to the realities of day-to-day life in the present.

Unhelpfully, the Constitution's Bill of Rights specifies only that "*Congress* [italics mine)] shall make no law respecting an establishment of religion… or the free exercise thereof." It fails to mention whether states also shouldn't, although some states did disestablish government-authorized and publicly funded churches. Often, though, the First Amendment's "Congress" stipulation had the likely unintended if inevitable effect that some states would continue, as they long had, their own coercive religious practices, such as creating official state churches and levying church taxes on all citizens, despite their private faiths.

For instance, the first Puritan settlers arriving in the New World in 1630 sought religious freedom for *their* faith but not for others; Virginia's official faith initially was the Church of England, and the government collected public taxes to support it (though Jefferson and other Founders in Virginia later led a successful campaign to abolish those practices). In addition, many colonial Christians in America, contrary to the Founding Fathers' fervent wishes, believed church-state power sharing was a good thing, as was previously a consensus assumption in Christian medieval Europe. Christine Leigh Heyrman, a professor of history at University of Delaware, wrote in an essay that in colonial Europe, "A majority of Protestants and Catholics alike believed that these *close* alliances between temporal and spiritual powers benefited both the church and the state by promoting individual morality, social harmony, and political stability."[9]

But the New World heralded a new age, and America was intended to be, governmentally if not culturally, an Enlightenment, humanist offspring.

The Founders' secularist desires were eventually seconded by the US Supreme Court—but more than 150 years after the Constitution was ratified. In 1947 Supreme Court Justice Hugo Black invoked Jefferson's phrase in the landmark *Everson vs. Board of Education* case, arguing that the "wall of separation" must be kept "high and impregnable."[10] It was the first case to rule that the Bill of Rights' "establishment" clause applied to states as well as the federal government.

Not that any of this has deterred committed Christians since the nation's founding from trying to evangelically insinuate their faith as deeply as possible into the warp and weft of American life, often targeting states and local schools. The hugely successful effects of this continuous stealth campaign since arrival of the so-called "Pilgrims," who, ironically considering how faithful things turned out, were mostly white settlers, not religious emigrants, has resulted in a country where overt signs of Christianity are literally everywhere. From Bibles in virtually every motel room (although that's changing); to new presidents pledging to protect the country by saying "So help me God," with their hand on a Bible; to Christmas, a national holiday for *all* Americans—Christians and non-Christian faithful and pagan outliers alike.

However, not *all* US presidents have recited inaugural oaths with a hand on the Bible. John Quincy Adams chose instead a book of law at his 1825 swearing in, but the historical record is thin for others (although Franklin Pierce and Lyndon Baines Johnson purportedly used alternative means).[11]

Why modern America remains so expansively and heretofore intractably Christian is enormously complicated, starting with understanding the history of why the first European Americans were mostly Christian by the time they first stepped ashore.

In brief, this is what happened:

- For reasons not yet fully understood by science, biological evolution naturally favored development of our highly imaginative human brains.
- We have for millennia used these brains to fervently imagine all manner of phantoms and all-powerful beings, and also, of particular relevance to this book, to worship them.
- Some energetic adherents after the death of Jesus Christ, notably the apostle Paul, successfully spread a nascent faith purporting that this prophet was both human and divine. But for several centuries, Christianity was widely viewed as but one crazy, dangerous cult among many trolling for converts in the Roman Empire.

- However, kind fate intervened early in the fourth century AD on behalf of the "Christians," as they were known: Roman Emperor Constantine, trying to ease intractable religious conflict in his realm, legalized the faiths of Christians and also of believers in other sects, which ended brutal persecutions that had threatened their survival and sharply limited their evangelical reach.
- Constantine ultimately proclaimed Christianity the official imperial religion and reportedly converted to the faith late in his life.
- With the fall of the Roman Empire late in the fifth century, virtually all classical, secular knowledge quickly vanished for most intents and purposes (as I noted in the Preface).
- For the next thousand years or so, Christian intellectual authority and reach increased exponentially as it exercised its near-absolute monopoly on knowledge. Its coercive power also surged in tandem with that of secular rulers as both collaborated to absolutely control the lives of their subjects.
- By the time English citizens—virtually all Christian by then—began emigrating to settle the New World and North America, the die had already been cast. And the modern result—a majority-Christian population in America—was all but guaranteed, although most colonial settlers were primarily motivated by envisioned riches in the here-and-now than immortality in the hereafter.

Still, virtually everyone in the new land was at least nominally Christian, so a Christian-infused cultural homogeneity evolved.

This helps explain why we Americans have remained so indelibly Christian over the nearly 250 years our nation has formally existed, even as supernatural ideas dissected by science have proven less and less credible—or even impossible—with each passing day. Let's consider what, if anything, might be done about that.

Part of the problem of explaining an obvious effect—the lion's share of twenty-first-century Americans remaining Christian—is the obscurity of its primordial root cause. Science confirms that our species' curiously instinctive tendency to imagine phantoms and believe they have agency (i.e., can purposefully and personally affect our lives) seems hardwired into our being. In our DNA, in other words. We intuitively often sense lions, not wind, hidden behind the waving grass. So, in a very real sense, we appear born to believe, in *something*. Modern studies in genetics and neurobiology have demonstrated innate human tendencies toward supernatural beliefs along with—unfortunately—behavioral instincts to automatically reject everything, no matter how undeniable, that seems to disprove those beliefs. Two books provide some good explanation of these concepts: *The God Gene*[12] by Dean Hamer and *The Republican Brain*[13] by Chris Mooney.

However, the fundamental problem that remains, particularly for doubters, skeptics, atheists, rationalists, humanists, and other miscellaneous unbelievers, is that the utter ubiquity of Christian belief in America does nothing to confirm the veracity of *what* is believed. It only proves that a whole lot of people in the nation, as throughout the world—billions of adherents, in fact—really, *really* believe it. But in the end, the only apparent "evidence" available to skeptics to allow a fair assessment of these spiritual assumptions are airy phantasms of mind, and human tendencies and impulses toward goodness that could logically be credited to our natural humanity and not divine intercession. Nonetheless, devout Christians believe their inward beliefs prove the authenticity of what they see as myriad outward manifestations of faith.

Still, the God of Christianity (singular or tripartite) for the moment rules the minds of a huge majority of Americans. It's simply a fact of life presently in the land of the free and home of the brave and devout. But this book is not about disabusing committed Christians from what may very well be just widely shared delusions—well, maybe it's a little about that—but rather to show how the faith organically took hold in the new land, rooted deeply in a brand-new environment, and refused to let go despite everything that material fate could inflict.

It's an impressive story but also a cautionary one, considering faith's manifest downsides, which have led humanists and fellow travelers to conclude that reality-based philosophies have a far better chance than supernatural imaginings of successfully lighting the paths of life, liberty, and happiness. Of course, the jury's still out.

In any event, the siren song of Christian faith appears to be steadily losing its appeal for Americans, as it has long since largely faded away in Western Europe.

The number of so-called "Nones," a demographic including atheists, agnostics, and those unaffiliated with any religious institutions or beliefs, has been sharply increasing in America (about 25 percent within the past couple of decades). These quasi-spiritual and doubtful souls now comprise about a quarter of the population—tens of millions of religious skeptics. And since young millennials (born roughly between 1980 and 1996) are predominantly irreligious, this trend will not only likely continue but quicken in the next few years.[14]

However, in the beginning, the Christian faith bloomed abundantly among European colonists in the New World as they sought to create a stable, nurturing environment conducive to survival, enrichment and, ultimately, conquest, while indigenous peoples were often brutalized in the process.

Let's investigate how it played out.

PART I

BEACHHEAD

"And here in Florida, Virginia, New-England, and Cannada, is more land than all the people in Christendome can manure, and yet more to spare than all the natives of those Countries can use and cultivate. The natives are only too happy to share."

— **Captain John Smith** (1580–1631),
first president of Jamestown, Virginia, governing council

CHAPTER 1

CONTACT

Jamestown starts the ball rolling in the New World

THE TERM "NEW World" is gloriously apt. Its discovery completely transformed humanity's common perception of our planet, the secrets it held, and even mankind's general sense of the outer boundaries of human possibility.

Before Italian mariner Christopher Columbus landed in October 1492 on what is now a Bahamian island in the Caribbean, some people still believed the world was flat, although the educated elite had long before surmised it was spherical, as the ancient Greeks had envisioned millennia before. But even top academics of the time initially believed Columbus had stumbled onto the eastern edge of Asia, not a separate continent theretofore unknown and unnamed. It is not even known if the master mariner really understood exactly what he had found by the time he died in 1506.

So what became known as the Age of Discovery began with the discovery that what the "Admiral of the Ocean Sea" had stumbled upon might be something completely new in Western history (although Scandinavian Vikings had very quietly visited the west coast of North America centuries earlier to far more muted effect). The name "America" derives from the Italian explorer Amerigo Vespucci, who during several voyages to the New World from 1499 to 1503 was the first to realize that the new land was not Asia but a new continent altogether.

Vespucci's voyages were part of a global exploration frenzy kickstarted decades earlier by the Dutch and then turbocharged by Columbus' transformative landing (financed by Spain's rulers who sought to profit from the discovery surge). European nations—predominantly England, France, Spain, the Netherlands, and Portugal—soon were dispatching fleets of sailing ships in every direction across the seven seas. European rulers were greedy for lands to colonize and economically exploit, indigenous gold to fill their royal vaults, and safer sea routes to the riches of China and India in the East (to avoid enemy Muslim domains overland). Frequently, if not always, the voyagers, particularly those bent on permanent colonial settlement, also brought missionaries to save souls for Christ.

Notably, earlier in the year of Columbus' first voyage west, Muslim Moors were expelled from Spain, their final Western European stronghold of the Middle Ages. The sense that Islam finally had been thrown out of Europe invigorated and emboldened Christians just as a brand-new world opened up to them. Indeed, Columbus himself hoped to convert Middle Eastern Muslims he mistakenly expected to meet in Asia as he traveled West.

Ironically, for years after Europeans first became aware of both New World continents (today identified as North and South America), they seemed less interested in exploring the strange, enormous land than quickly profiting from its lush agricultural potential, and its gold, silver, and furs. Alternately, they longed to find a route past the Americas to the wealth of Asia. But for nearly a century after the first of Columbus' four westward voyages, most of the action remained in and around North and South America. Portuguese mariner Ferdinand Magellan's crew's epic circumnavigation of the globe in 1519 to 1522 (Magellan was killed in a local quarrel in the Philippines in 1521) proved that no easy route existed through the New World to Asia. In fact, it showed Asia could only be reached by traversing an astonishingly vast ocean (the Pacific), and then only *after* getting past the seemingly endless Americas.

A number of British explorers in the 1500s had investigated lands and waters in proximity to what would become eastern Canada, notably in Newfoundland and along the St. Lawrence estuary, a Great Lakes outlet into the

Atlantic Ocean via North America's St. Lawrence River. Briton Sir Francis Drake explored the west coast of North America and the shoreline of Peru in South America.

Eventually, in 1585, British colonists came ashore in what would become, about two centuries later, the United States.

ROANOKE

When English privateers sent by Sir Walter Raleigh arrived on August 18, 1590, at a small Atlantic coast fort on Roanoke Island in what is now North Carolina, they were stunned.

No one was there.

Some five years earlier, another Raleigh expedition had built the fort, storage buildings, and some dwellings, and, before returning to England, left 107 people (men and a few women and children) to establish a viable colony at the site. A bad omen immediately preceded Raleigh's departure from Roanoke: His men reportedly burned an Indian village over a stolen silver cup. In the next several years, mishaps scuttling various Roanoke resupply voyages plus Spain's invasion of England effectively marooned and apparently doomed the fledgling colony.

Queen Elizabeth I had chartered Roanoke colony to settle and exploit New World land, find gold and other wealth, and attack Spanish shipping in the region.

Among the colonists reportedly missing when Roanoke Gov. John White returned to resupply the outpost in the late summer of 1590 were his daughter Ellinor Dare and his granddaughter Virginia, the first English child born in America. The only clue to the inhabitants' disappearance was the word "CROATOAN"—the name of an island some fifty miles away—carved in a fence post. But no one was found there when the sailors went to investigate.[15]

Archaeologists reported in 1998 that tree-ring data revealed extreme drought conditions persisted in Virginia between 1587 and 1589, which they believed may have hastened the demise of the already resource-starved Roanoke colony.[16]

The failed venture became known to history as "The Lost Colony," and the fate of the missing colonists is still unknown.

JAMESTOWN

Seventeen years later, in 1607, the English made a second attempt to colonize America's east coast. The entire coastal area, from Florida north, was then known as Virginia, after the unmarried "Virgin Queen," Elizabeth.

One hundred colonists on three ships—the *Susan Constant, Godspeed* and *Discovery*—reached Chesapeake Bay in April and immediately began searching for a suitable settlement site. The adventurers ultimately agreed on a site in a narrow peninsula on the James River, going ashore there May 14.

Importantly, as would the "Pilgrims" later, the colonists first established a governing council before searching for a final site. Commander Christopher Newport and John Smith, a former mercenary captain, were to be the leaders. The fledgling colony, known at various times as James Forte, James Towne, and James Cittie—eventually Jamestown—initially included a triangular fort, church, storehouse, and housing.

Jamestown almost didn't make it. Taking two ships and forty crewmen, Capt. Newport returned that summer to England for supplies and to report to the queen. But the colonists who remained in the new settlement were thereafter ravaged by hunger and disease and the constant worry of Indian attack. Upon his return in early 1608, Smith negotiated an agreement with the powerful local chief, Powhatan, allowing the colonists to trade beads, metal tools (including weapons), and other items to neighboring tribes for foodstuffs like corn. Life in Jamestown then markedly improved.

But the newfound ease didn't last. After Smith left for England in late 1609, more than one hundred settlers died in the long, brutally cold winter. Just as the last destitute colonists verged on abandoning the settlement in the spring of the following year, two ships unexpectedly arrived with 150 colonists and the colony's new governor, Lord De La Warr.

After shortly falling ill, De La Warr soon headed back to England and was replaced by Sir Thomas Gates. The new governor quickly instituted strict laws that enforced discipline in the community and implemented stern militarist policies against the Algonquin Indian tribes in the area. Indian villages were raided, indigenous inhabitants slain, and their homes and crops burned. The atrocities betrayed the Indians' generosity in transferring life-sustaining knowledge to the colonists, such as how to insulate their huts in winter with naturally available materials and how to successfully grow the Algonquin's main staple crop: corn (which the Indians called *maize*).

But fate smiled on Jamestown in 1619 when local colonist John Rolfe, a planter, married Indian princess Pocahontas, a daughter of powerful Powhatan who had been captured by the English and reportedly embraced Christianity. (In published writings about his colonial experiences, John Smith claimed, perhaps apocryphally, that when he had been a captive of the Algonquin chief and due to be executed in 1607, Pocahontas intervened with her father to save his life.)

The Jamestown economy thrived after Rolfe introduced a particularly bountiful strain of West Indian tobacco to the area. Also in 1619, the first Africans arrived in Jamestown after being poached from a Portuguese slave ship captured in the Caribbean. Since the New World's ignoble slave system wouldn't develop for many years hence, it's likely that the initial fifty African men, women, and children who arrived in Jamestown were initially indentured to pick tobacco there, not enslaved.

After Pocahontas and Powhatan died, in 1617 and 1618, respectively, relations between settlers and Indians deteriorated. Colonist land grabs and aggressive behavior, plus Old World diseases that proved lethal to Indians, fueled Algonquin resentments against the newcomers. In March 1622, Indian warriors attacked English settlements in Virginia, killing 350 to four hundred people, about a fourth of the frontier's population at that time. Jamestown itself, benefitting from advance warning and a defensive system, weathered the onslaught, but many outlying settlements and plantations were decimated.

Years of settler-Indian conflict continued through 1644, but the Algonquin were ultimately defeated and forced to sign a treaty with the English that appropriated most of their land and exacted an annual tribute. When Jamestown's central statehouse burned down in 1698, Williamsburg was selected to replace it as Virginia's colonial capital. The original Jamestown fort later disappeared in history.

THE PURITAN CONNECTION

Interestingly, religion appeared not to be a major motivator for either the Roanoke or Jamestown colonists themselves, who were mostly adventurers and wealth seekers, although Puritan financiers provided capital for the ventures.

English Puritans were basically scripturally nitpicking Anglican Calvinists, and early in the seventeen century they began to conflict with fellow Anglicans who adopted Arminianism (and the government who increasingly supported them). The Arminian theology proposed that salvation could be obtained by human will and acceptance of God's saving grace through individual resistance to innate sinfulness. Puritans, on the other hand, believed that man was irremediably and irresistibly sinful and could only be saved if *specifically* and arbitrarily "elected" by God for salvation. In other words, for Puritans, people could do nothing to ensure their own salvation except possibly catch the eye of the divine by living a manifestly holy life and hoping to be tapped as one of his elect.

England's joint-stock Virginia Company was created to develop English colonies in the New World in an area now known as New England, and some of its key financiers were, incidentally, Puritan devotees. The company funded the Jamestown settlement, which shakily survived with little profit until 1620, when America's first overtly Christian community was founded in what is now Massachusetts by colonists known as the "Pilgrims." "The Great Migration," a historic mass exodus of English Puritans to America, began in 1630 with the arrival of the first batch of faithful families in John Winthrop's fleet. Some twenty thousand more Puritans made the trip in the next ten years.

The Virginia Company went out of business in 1624, but the ethos it established—the right to self-government of American colonies, bestowed by the English king—lived on. This special freedom presaged the birth of American democracy.

While international politics drove the Roanoke project and profit-lusting greed fueled the Jamestown dream, religion didn't overtly enter the migratory equation until the so-called Pilgrims. A decade later the holy impulse surged with the Puritan rush, whose stated aim was to establish a godly commonwealth in the new land where Puritans could worship as they pleased without interference.

"[O]ut of small beginnings greater things have been produced... as one small candle may light a thousand..."

— **William Bradford** (1590–1657),
a signatory of the Pilgrim's seminal Mayflower Compact and intermittent governor of Plymouth Colony for thirty years

CHAPTER 2

CHRISTIANITY ARRIVES IN AMERICA

Protestant reformists plant first enduring settlement

WHEN THE TINY *Mayflower* reached the New World in the winter of 1620, it made first landfall on the northern tip of what is now Cape Cod, today a Massachusetts icon of beachy American upper- and upper-middle-class contentment.

The vessel brought with it particularly zealous Protestant believers, the first to purposely export an ethos of non-Catholic piety to the new land, and one that would color America's global reputation into modern times. Catholic missionaries by this time had already been active for a while in New England, Canada, Florida, Georgia, and into the New Mexico territories, and Spanish Franciscan friars were beginning to set up missions in California.

Because the vast majority of newcomers to the New World in its early years were at least nominally Christian—although many were also zealots (as were many on the *Mayflower*)—the faith gained an important foothold in America during its emergent years.

The *Mayflower* emigrants were descendants of the European religious upheaval known as the Reformation, which several decades after Columbus' landfall in the New World had begun to force a permanent and cataclysmic split in Western Christianity. The rift was between traditional Catholics under papal authority and upstart Protestants inspired by renegade German Catholic priest Martin Luther. Protestants believed in the literal truth of scripture, not Catholic ritual and dogma, and in a modest personal God, not the gold-dripping extravagances of Catholicism and its pope, whom they viewed as unholy and dictatorial.

The so-called "Pilgrims" were religious as well as political exiles to the New World. They sought sanctuary from persecution by the dominant Church of England (a Protestant denomination that retained some ornate trappings of Catholicism) as well as English King James I's government. Church and state both mistrusted the sect and collaborated to oppress it.

The Reformation turned once-monolithic Western Catholicism into a Christian hodgepodge of Catholics and Protestants, sometimes putting even officially Catholic nations (like France and Spain) at odds, creating conflict among Protestant nations with different Christian practices, and ripping chasms within individual nations as multiple versions of Christianity fought each other.

For persecuted European Christians, the New World offered a new day. When the English faithful arrived in what would one day become the United States of America, the only religious tradition to be found was aboriginal.

Although the Plymouth Colony founded by the *Mayflower* emigrants was the second surviving mainland English colony in British North America, after Jamestown, the Christian "Pilgrim" theme acquired a paramount focus in American history and culture. But its almost mythological status in American consciousness didn't coalesce until many years after the landing at Plymouth Rock. Keep in mind that the Bermuda Colony, for which sugar was king, predated the Plymouth Colony.

It's interesting to note that Protestant Christianity was in reality just a historical happenstance in the New World's early colonization, not a cohesive plan. Indeed, as we shall see, over time the colonial American population—as well as its religious sects—grew impressively diverse if still mostly Christian. But colonial religion was never a homogenous tableau; spiritually apathetic and even disdainful colonists—non-Christian and nominally Christian alike—were liberally sprinkled among the more numerous faithful. Despite the ostensible religious liberty the new land encouraged, diversity of religious sects in the colonies, paradoxically, was the precise cause of constant internecine friction.

Whereas people with Protestant leanings comprised a significant (likely majority) presence in the republic's early years, that status slowly eroded (today only about 46 percent of Americans identify as Protestants). In nascent colonial times, however, Protestants flooded in, mainly from England and Germany initially. Several of the thirteen original colonies were founded by specific religious sects: for example, Puritans (a.k.a. Congregationalists) in Massachusetts, as we've seen; British Quakers in Pennsylvania; Catholics in Maryland (although their majority eventually eroded); and English Anglicans (of the Church of England) in Virginia.

FEDERAL VERSUS STATE

Notably, the Constitution decreed only that that the *federal government* could make no laws regarding establishment of religion but did not mention states, as I mentioned earlier. As late as the 1830s, one state—Massachusetts—still provided public tax funds to its Congregational churches. Laws were also eventually passed and effective up to the American Revolution favoring Protestants in immigration to the colonies, requiring a profession of Christian faith and prescribing lengths of residency for citizenship. But this was political more than religious; the English king wanted fealty from colonists, and he believed Protestants—England was officially Protestant—were most to be trusted in that regard.

Yet the flood of newcomers to the New World would, in fact, prove a religiously technicolor bunch.

America's colonial citizenry eventually ranged from British, German, and Scandinavian Protestants to French, Spanish, and Portuguese Catholics, to Deists, radical Anabaptists (such as the Amish and Hutterite sects), Jews, Hindus, Voodoo practitioners from the Caribbean, Native American animists, and even Satan worshippers, among many other faiths and spiritual inclinations. Not to mention African slaves who brought their traditional faiths with them on New World-bound slave ships. The new land even contained prominent skeptics, such as colonial atheist firebrand Thomas Paine and, of course, fire-and-brimstone Christian zealots. Many others were just uninspired by if not altogether antagonistic toward faith of any kind.

In religion, as in everything else, early America was a "melting pot," a phenomenon so true it became a cliché. That fact more than any—our unique brand of homogeneity born of diversity—is what ultimately colored the American experience. It also deeply informs our American habits, institutions, laws and values that have organically evolved over centuries into the modern era.

But the Christianizing ostensibly began, as every American child learns early, with the "Pilgrims."

THE 'PILGRIMS'

The *Mayflower* band succeeded in establishing the third enduring colonial community in the new land after Jamestown (and, peripherally, the offshore Caribbean plantation colony in Bermuda), and possibly more tellingly, the first infused with Christian piety.

Contrary to popular belief, the iconic *Mayflower* wasn't the only ship bearing English pilgrims that set sail from England in 1620 bound for the New World. Initially, there were actually two sister vessels—the *Mayflower* and the smaller *Speedwell*—which were not filled with "Pilgrims," the term commonly accepted in American historiography, but, technically, Brownists (and others).

To clarify, the difference between Brownist "Pilgrims" (named after Robert Browne, the English founder of the sect), and later Puritans (both nominally Anglican) is that the latter simply sought to *reform* the Church of England, whereas the former viewed that church body as irredeemable and sought to *separate* from it. But both Puritans and Brownists were exceptionally pious and righteous for the day.

The separatist Brownists, unlike the Jamestown group of mostly male entrepreneurs seeking wealth, were religious pilgrims who first fled persecution in England to the more liberal Netherlands. But finding day-to-day existence and making a living among mistrusting aliens in Holland too daunting, many in the sect ultimately decided to emigrate to the seductively free Americas. A Harvard American history scholar I consulted for this book noted the amusing irony that the Pilgrims—a group of people reviled in their own country of England and then so disliked in their adopted home of the Netherlands that they fled to the New World—"ended up becoming the founding myth of the United States!"

For the next two hundred years, these intrepid emigrants were to be commonly known as Brownists, not Pilgrims, and their journey was most commonly referred to as the Brownist Emigration. The debut use of the term "Pilgrims" in describing the most devout *Mayflower* passengers was in first Plymouth colony leader William Bradford's journal written between 1630 and 1651 (he spelled it "pilgrimes"). But more than a century and a half passed before it would come into common usage.

By the departure of the *Mayflower* and *Speedwell*, non-English colonization of both Americas (North and South) and the Caribbean was already well underway. In North America at the time, Dutch Protestant colonization was evolving in the New Netherland area (ultimately New York), and Spanish Catholic communities were emerging in future Florida and New Mexico. Other Catholic holdings dotted New France, along the northeastern St. Lawrence River, in what would become Canada. Catholic Spain and Portugal were also colonizing vast expanses of Central and South America.

So, the Brownists were but a tiny drop on a huge stain of colonization spreading westward over the globe by the seventeenth century, and they were relative latecomers at that. Spain, which bankrolled Columbus' voyages, since 1492 had been energetically colonizing vast areas in the New World, and Catholic France started exploring territories in 1534. Portugal began colonizing Brazil in 1500, and the Netherlands and Sweden also founded colonies in America starting early in the seventeenth century. Thus, while most of the areas that would eventually comprise the US were majority Protestant in early colonial times; colonists in areas beyond (e.g., in what is now Canada and Mexico) were largely Catholic.

Yet, the tiny dissident Brownist group succeeded in founding the second English colony on mainland North America (after Jamestown) and the first sizeable English settlement in New England. They named their colonial village Plymouth (after their departure port in England). What makes the

Plymouth colony special, certainly, is its historical reputation as a haven for Puritan Pilgrims, upper case, but, as we'll see, not pilgrims, lower case, of *other* religious sects. Perhaps it is honored more for the *ad hoc* democratic document the colonists created to assure justice and peace within the group: the Mayflower Compact.

Plymouth would become the oldest continuously inhabited, sizeable settlement in America, and the community generated a powerful, creative motif for the future nation that spread from it. The emerging nation, especially early on and particularly on the eastern seaboard, tended to generally adapt the Plymouth model, where communities' social and legal norms were greatly informed by English customs, Christian values, and Calvinist order. However, this was leavened overall by a purported tremendous amount of "Wild West"-style debauchery and decidedly un-Christian behavior in less-structured new communities further inland, on frontiers and, truth be told, even in Puritan strongholds as well (read Nathaniel Hawthorne's 1850 classic *The Scarlet Letter: A Romance*). Other Protestant sects, including the Anglophile Anglicans that ultimately dominated Virginia and Evangelicals in Tennessee and Kentucky, presented a broad mix of religious and cultural norms in the early colonies.

But the Brownists did not embed the ethos of religious tolerance in the budding nation, as many Americans assume; it was their fledgling proto-democracy that ultimately set them apart. In truth, as we shall see, the colonial America that evolved from Plymouth Colony was, at least initially and before the Constitution was written, nothing if not *opposed* to religious freedom. At least within each sect's own sphere of influence. Later on, though, some minority denominations championed religious liberty for all Americans as a path to ensuring their own spiritual freedom.

It's true that the Brownists had at one time fled religious oppression and thus presumably well understood the ugliness of persecution, but their journey to America was more religiously self-centered than tolerantly inclusive of others.

GOING TO AMERICA

The two Brownist ships left Southampton, England, for America about July 5, 1620, with 120 passengers combined. Roughly a third of those onboard were Brownists, who expedition member William Bradford, a separatist himself who ultimately became governor of Plymouth Colony, referred to as "Saints,"[17] and their children. Another group, described as "The Strangers" (from a biblical reference from the phrase "strangers and pilgrimes" used in Bradford's journal) were non-separatist tradesmen and servants hired by the Merchant Adventurer company, the venture's financier. Merchant Adventurer agents were included in the group to govern and provide manpower for the new colony; these included appointed military commander Miles Standish and governor-designee Stephen Hopkins (replaced later by William Bradford). Captains and crew rounded out the list of travelers.

The group's departure from England had been delayed for a month due to disagreements with Merchant Adventurers. The holdup proved deadly.

Once finally afloat, the ships still didn't get far. The flotilla had to turn back twice when the *Speedwell* began leaking badly. Ultimately, the *Speedwell* was judged unseaworthy, and passengers who did not then abandon the trip altogether joined the *Mayflower* party.

On September 16, the hundred-foot-long *Mayflower,* now with 102 passengers and about thirty crew onboard, set sail for the Americas. Their supplies eroded by delay, the passengers were already exhausted from disappointments, tedium, and postponement, and winter dangerously approached. The first month was relatively calm on the Atlantic, but as winter gales battered the small ship during the next, two passengers died.

On November 21, after sixty-six days at sea, the modest craft made landfall in what became known as Provincetown Harbor (now Provincetown, Massachusetts) inside the tip of hook-shaped Cape Cod peninsula. Powerful Atlantic tempests had initially prevented the ship from going further south to its intended destination in the Colony of Virginia near what is now New York. That is where the Pilgrims were officially authorized by royal charter to establish a settlement. Further attempts to move south were battered by inclement weather and shipwreck-threatening rocks.

So the group's leaders ultimately decided instead to find an unauthorized spot to settle in the Cape area.

After encountering hostile Nauset Indians on "First Encounter Beach," the colonists' initial temporary landfall in the New World in early November, they decided to look for a more hospitable site on the mainland. Indian enmity was the sour fruit from earlier encounters with random European traders and explorers who had committed atrocities against them after coming ashore. So the natives the *Mayflower* colonists encountered were not welcoming. After reboarding the ship, crew and passengers traveled on, eventually encountering the Plymouth site.

THE MAYFLOWER COMPACT

Initially, many Saints were worried about the legality of settling in an area lacking royal authorization or a formal governing code. They disagreed with the Strangers, who threatened to go it alone and "use their owne libertie," as a worried Bradford phrased it. So in an effort to calm concerns and maintain unity, the colonists cooperatively created the Mayflower Compact. The historic document was signed the day after Christmas, before landing at a selected site on the mainland, which would become Plymouth. The voyagers were well aware that ineffective government had doomed earlier colonial enterprises in the Americas.

The two-hundred-word Compact became a seminal document for the American experiment, binding its signers (forty-one male passengers—women at the time were not allowed to vote) to form a consensus government and to abide by any laws and regulations later established "for the general good of the colony." The Compact was not a constitution nor a religious document per se but "an adaptation of a Puritan church covenant to a civil situation."[18] It proved to be an effective blueprint for their common civic governance and remained operative until the colony joined *Massachusetts Bay Colony* in 1691. And it was an important precursor in the evolution of American democracy.

The Compact assumed the settlers' allegiance to the king, the accepted practice at the time. The signers viewed the document as temporary, a stopgap until the Council of New England could grant permanency to the group's settlement. That authorization came in 1621 with the Pierce Patent.

Still, the Compact manifestly proved that colonists far from British authority in a distant land could govern themselves by their own rules, if necessary, irrespective of English law. And because the Pilgrims' innovative document was at heart a jury-rigged Christian congregational blueprint, it necessarily embedded religious sensibilities into secular governance where it was adapted, and likewise served to spread Christianity in the colonies—and ultimately throughout America—in a self-perpetuating form.

It's important to note that early on in the New World, the only organized governing institution in many small towns and hamlets was the local Christian church, and pastors were often communities' most influential leaders.

WINTER OF DISCONTENT

The Brownists' first winter in the New World was devastating. Sometimes several colonists would die in a single day. Tragically, because the colonists had arrived too late in the year to build many huts (only seven of nineteen planned residences and four common houses were built during the cold months), many of the settlers were forced to remain huddled on the *Mayflower*, often shivering in extremely cramped, drafty, and uninsulated quarters.

Bradford wrote in a memoir that not everyone showed Christian charity during that hard winter, some ignoring the pleas of those who began to die. But, still, he said many saints, often weak and sick themselves, labored to ease the suffering of others. Some such "Good Samaritans" died in the process. At one point, reportedly fewer than ten saints were well enough to nurse the sick.

The women, children, and infirm did not step off the ship for months. As the winter dragged on, contagious disease, malnutrition, and unavoidable exposure to the brutal, alien New England cold killed half the passengers and crew, all woefully unprepared for the weather. Thirteen of the expedition's eighteen women died that winter. Come spring, only fifty-three passengers remained alive, many just barely, but as more huts were built more colonists were able to disembark.

Some encouraging progress, however, marked the first warming months. A few *Mayflower* men were healthy enough in February to drag six cannons up a nearby hill to protect against feared Indian attacks, and the settlement was thus well defended. Then in March a treaty was successfully negotiated with the local *Wampanoag* Indian chief, Massasoit, bringing temporary security to the fledgling colony.

In May 1621, Capt. Christopher Jones piloted the *Mayflower* on its return voyage to England with only a skeleton crew of survivors, but nonetheless the craft made the return crossing in half the time of the original journey.

A different ship, though also named *Mayflower*, sailed in 1629 from London to Plymouth Colony carrying thirty-five passengers, many from the original Pilgrims' former congregation in Leiden. The ship also traveled to America in 1630, 1633, 1634, and 1639. Sadly, it vanished with its 140 passengers on a trip to Virginia in 1641.[19] This vessel also reportedly conducted trade between Massachusetts, the Caribbean West Indies and Africa, and on at least one occasion transported African slaves to the New World.[20]

THANKSGIVING

The traditional Thanksgiving harvest festival, long observed as a national holiday in the United States, is believed to stem from a celebratory harvest gathering in October 1621. Celebrants included the fifty-three Pilgrim survivors of the first hard winter along with Chief Massasoit and ninety of his men. Three extant accounts of the event indicate that the celebration lasted three days and featured feasts of waterfowl and fish provided by the colonists and venison brought by the Indians.[21] Other accounts indicate that most people ate in the open air (Plymouth still had few buildings), and the men shot firearms, ran foot races, drank liquor, and struggled to communicate in a muddle of broken English, the Wampanoag tongue, and sign language.

It was a fruitful gathering but, unfortunately, it succeeded in sealing only a temporary, if long, honeymoon between the settlers and Wampanoag. The tribe provided critical corn seed to plant the following spring and other provisions necessary for the colonists' survival.

The hopeful détente lasted until the Pequot War (1636–1638), in which

Massachusetts, Plymouth, and Saybrook colonists and their Narragansett and Mohegan allies decisively defeated Connecticut's Pequot tribe, killing or enslaving about seven hundred Pequot Indians.[22] This catastrophe was followed by King Philip's War (1675–1676), in which hundreds of colonists and thousands of Indians in the Plymouth area perished.

"For we must Consider that we shall be as a City upon a Hill, the eyes of all people are upon us; so that if we shall deal falsely with our god in this work we have undertaken and so cause him to withdraw his present help from us, we shall be made a story and a byword through the world, we shall open the mouths of enemies to speak evil of the ways of god..."

— **John Winthrop** (1587/88–1649),
a founder and nineteen-term governor of
Massachusetts Bay Colony

CHAPTER 3

A 'CITY UPON A HILL'

American Christianity gets organized

WHEN JOHN WINTHROP and nearly one thousand English Puritans in eleven ships came ashore in New England in June 1630 and founded a settlement in what is now Boston, they delivered a viral cargo of rigid Calvinist/Puritan-style Christian piety to the New World.

One of the ideas they brought with them was a biblically prescribed view that God helps those who help themselves, that poverty is a kind of sin, the result of a *willful* failure to work and thrive. That cruel idea is with us still. Forty-six percent of all Christians today generally blame poverty on an individual lack of effort, compared with 29 percent of non-Christians, according to a 2017 survey by the *Washington Post* and Kaiser Family Foundation. The bias is even more pronounced among Evangelicals (53 percent) and Catholics (50 percent).[23]

In his groundbreaking book, *The Protestant Ethic and the Spirit of Capitalism*, Max Weber (1864–1920) credited ascetic Protestantism with a critical role in unleashing the driving spirit of modern capitalism, as I fundamentally link early colonial religiosity to how American culture evolved overall into the twenty-first century.

Weber argues that early American Calvinism, with its concept of an elite "elect" among Christian faithful specifically chosen by God for immortality, encouraged a sense that personal prosperity strongly indicated divine favor. American Christians obsessively began seeking clues to their elect-ness, Weber believed. An excellent summary of the book in SparkNotes states:

> Weber argues that this new attitude broke down the traditional economic system, paving the way for modern capitalism. However, once capitalism emerged, the Protestant values were no longer necessary, and their ethic took on a life of its own. We are now locked into the spirit of capitalism because it is so useful for modern economic activity.[24]

But, this religio-economic transformation was not instantaneous.

TOUGH GOING

At first it was tough going for America's first Puritan immigrants in the Winthrop fleet. Many died en route to the New World, and another two hundred, including Winthrop's son Henry, reportedly perished, mostly from disease, during their early months in the New World. But Winthrop swallowed his personal grief and threw himself into his holy work, laboring beside servants and other workers to set a good example against idleness for novice colonists.

As the new colony developed, it experimented with democratic governing principles. It gradually required church membership for voting *freemen*, thus securing later-troublesome connective tissue between church and state. Winthrop ultimately served as colonial governor for ten of the colony's first twenty years and nine as lieutenant governor.

Although Winthrop was a force for relative moderation in the religiously conservative colony, he was no "liberal democrat" in the modern sense. He opposed attempts to expand voting and civil rights in the colony, preferring governance by an elite, and in fact called democracy "the meanest and worst of all forms of government," which was a common notion of the elite in Winthrop's day.

Despite writing a famous sermon entitled "A Modell of Christian Charity," he was notably uncharitable, in an ethical sense, to heterodox preachers

Roger Williams and Anne Hutchinson (although his followers would have applauded him). Williams and Hutchinson questioned Puritan doctrines of salvation by good works and also the sect's treatment of Native Americans. Both naysayers were eventually banished from the colony.

That Winthrop himself was opposed to democratic ideas did not stop others in the colony from eventually forcing the issue. Ironically, a compromise that evolved between the colony's more progressive and more conservative factions was a precursor to the future American system of government—but with religious fine print.

At first, although the colony's founding charter required that the governor, deputy governor, and eighteen assistant magistrates be elected by all Massachusetts freemen, for several years an ostensibly temporary council of eight filled all those positions. When a large number of non-Puritan immigrants arrived in 1633 to 1634, they joined other skeptical colonists in demanding to see the colony's original charter.

Winthrop opposed any election procedural change and a secret ballot but agreed to these after convincing electors of each town to send only two post-election representatives to sit on the governing council. He believed, sensibly, that legislating with every single freeman in congress would be cumbersome and unworkable. Ironically, Winthrop lost the 1634 election to an ally who also disapproved of voting changes, Thomas Dudley.

Still, the colony's majority religion fundamentally influenced its governance. To be a legal elector, each freeman in the new, ostensibly more democratic elections was still required to undergo rigorous scrutiny of his Puritan religious beliefs and to be a formal member of a recognized church in the colony. Indeed, Winthrop and other magistrates rejected a petition to allow all Englishmen in the colony to be electors, not just the church-affiliated. Authorities even fined and jailed the main petitioners.

BILL OF RIGHTS PRECURSOR

In 1641, also against Winthrop's wishes, the governing council passed the Massachusetts Body of Liberties, one of the first documents protecting individual rights in America and a precursor to the future nation's constitutional Bill of Rights.

Some of the liberties specified in this document explicitly cited sources in Christian scripture, including a justification for slavery, upon which the colony became heavily dependent. Although when Americans think of antebellum slavery, they generally think of the "peculiar institution" as it existed in the Southern states, but it flourished in colonial America in the North as well, even as many disapproving New Englanders held their noses but still took profits from it, directly and indirectly.

Puritanism's legacy in America—from stern but comforting piety to the Salem Witch Trials—is mixed. As political scientist Matthew Holland contends, Winthrop "is at once a significant founding father of America's best and worst impulses," his vigorous promotion of charity and community degraded by what Holland considered unbending intolerance and punitive, judgmental acts.[25]

The Puritan faith—which social critic H.L. Mencken sarcastically dismissed as imbued with "the haunting fear that someone, somewhere, may be happy"—derived from Calvinism. A French anti-Catholic reformist scholar, Calvin in 1536 founded a super-organized Protestant society in Geneva, Switzerland that proved enormously successful and politically powerful. Calvinism was initially dismissed as heresy by Lutherans (the Protestant reform sect of Martin Luther that sparked the Reformation) and considered itself a reform version of Lutheranism.

Calvinists believed that people were eligible for salvation by faith in God alone, not good works, but that only "elect" persons God arbitrarily chooses will ultimately be saved. So, believers then had no way of knowing whether they would be saved in the end. The sect also believed that Jesus is not physically present in the eucharist (as opposed to Lutherans), that God is part of a divine trinity and that the Bible is the divinely inspired, unerring source of the "word of God."

However, perhaps more influential to America's evolution was the rigid

Christian social system Calvin embedded within the Swiss state. The Puritans then transplanted that almost geometric system and its intractably pious ethos in America.

'SOMBER CRANKS AND KILLJOYS'

When Winthrop introduced to the New World his first Puritans—"somber cranks and kill-joys," as one historian indelicately described them[26]—he immediately set to work to transplant the same rigid social/religious Protestant system that Calvin had successfully implanted in Geneva, Switzerland, in the 1500s.

Calvin believed people's day-to-day lives should be strictly ordered according to biblical precepts—"order" being the operative concept. Historian David Hall believed that "the intellectual descendants of Calvin were the founders of colonial America,"[27] and historian John T. McNeill wrote that both Plymouth and Massachusetts Bay colonies were "definitely Calvinist."[28] In Massachusetts, Winthrop ignored other traditional Protestant texts, exclusively distributing Calvin's "Geneva Bible," a collection of doctrinal documents, including Calvin's own influential and self-written *Institutes of the Christian Religion*, various psalms for singing (some authored by Calvin), and other lesser spiritual literature.

Calvin had instituted a strict hierarchical system in Geneva prescribing tiered levels of authority for each congregation and assigning church officials to live widely dispersed among the communities of faithful to more closely monitor families' piety and behavior. Multiple weekly sermons were scheduled and attendance was mandatory, and a historian I know told me (although I couldn't find any corroboration online), that some churches employed staff known as "pokers," who would jab people in pews who fell asleep during sermons. Calvinist churches also ensured that children were rigorously indoctrinated in the faith through church activities.

At the end of his life, Calvin not only had complete authority over his flock's spiritual life but also, with his enormous influence in Geneva's city government, he controlled much of believers' temporal existence as well. He personally approved executions for heresy.

During the 1630s, some twenty thousand English Puritans immigrated to America, usually in families and most settling in New England, as royal and mainstream Anglican persecution of the sect in England became untenable. The Puritan ethos quickly caught hold and spread in New England but not as much elsewhere, at least initially.

However, despite the controlling influence of the Puritans' regimented church-state system in Massachusetts in the seventeenth century, America elsewhere steadily grew more and more religiously diverse in the coming decades.

The nation's Puritan influence also has had rhetorical "legs," as it were. The elevated tone of Christian piety and freedom in Winthrop's sermons and other writings continue to inspire US politicians even today. Such modern political luminaries as John F. Kennedy, Ronald Reagan, Barak Obama, even Sarah Palin, have referenced Calvin. Winthrop also makes a cameo fictional appearance in Nathaniel Hawthorne's classic Gothic novel of Puritan terror, *The Scarlet Letter*. Winthrop's familial descendants include former presidential candidate and US Secretary of State John Kerry, who was raised Catholic, but whose paternal grandparents were Austro-Hungarian Jewish immigrants to America who converted to Catholicism. Although Kerry's mother was an Episcopalian, his father was Catholic.

Thus, while the spiritual path of American immigrants zigged and zagged in many spiritual (even atheistic) directions once the newcomers arrived in the new land—they either kept their religion, found a new one or lost faith altogether—Christianity soon became the nation's majority faith by far, as it remains today.

"*America owes most of its social prejudices to the exaggerated religious opinions of the different sects which were so instrumental in establishing the colonies.*"

— **James Fenimore Cooper** (1789–1851),
author of the classic American novel,
The Last of the Mohicans

CHAPTER 4

BABEL

A cacophony of belief

AFTER THE FOUNDING of Plymouth and other fledgling colonies in America, the new land's broad religious diversity, though still largely Christian, grew apparent.

European immigrants to North America during the Reformation and Enlightenment were frequently Protestants seeking to escape Catholic domination in areas where Old World Catholicism still reigned supreme or was brutally trying to reinforce its primacy. The newcomers were mainly Anglicans, Baptists, Congregationalists, Presbyterians, Lutherans, Quakers, Mennonites, and Moravians. But there was also a fair amount of Catholic migration to the New World, as well, as Catholic Spain, Portugal, and France energetically planted colonies and converted natives in parts of what would become Canada, Florida, Arizona, New Mexico, and California.

INDIGENOUS FAITH

And, of course, the newcomers found indigenous people in the Americas and Caribbean who worshipped in ways both alien and familiar. The Algonquin people on the eastern seaboard, for example, were dualists. Like Descartes and Plato, they believed that souls and bodies were separate, that inanimate objects like stones have souls, and that humans can access supernatural realms in dreams. Dreams were therefore sacred to the Algonquin, how "gods make known their will to men."[29]

Due to the religious-pilgrim DNA of early American colonists, there was undoubtedly a surfeit of Christian piety and devotion around, but scholars also note a fair amount of religious apathy in the New World up to the American Revolution, as well as outright warfare among sects.

Then, as now, many faithful—even regular churchgoers—knew little of the contents of the Bible and were often illiterate and ill-equipped to fully understand them even if they did read. Indeed, colonial women were generally only semi-literate if at all (education of women was considered unnecessary), including Benjamin Franklin's own sister. Plus, the colonies were plagued by all manner of scarcity, including a shortage of ordained clergy.

So, religion was clearly a hit-or-miss affair in colonial days, depending on your family upbringing, personal spiritual propensities, proximity to church and churchmen, and the religious texture of your community—should you even have a community. Fur trappers or frontiersmen, for example, were often marooned in heathen wilderness far from any formal word of God.

Although most colonists were Christian, Protestants and Catholics were often in conflict due to inherited animosities from their long and pitched struggles in Europe. Spanish, Portuguese, and French Catholics fought intramurally against one another as well.

SECTARIAN VIOLENCE

In the first major sectarian conflict between Europeans in what would become the United States, Spanish Catholic colonists from a fort at St. Augustine in modern-day Florida massacred Huguenots (French Protestants) in 1564 at nearby Fort Caroline (now Jacksonville). The next year, on a Florida beach, Spaniards slaughtered survivors of a shipwrecked French immigrant fleet.[30]

Nonetheless, early America was an overflowing cornucopia of immigrant European peoples who gave the colonies their unique spiritual environment. The newcomers arrived with their stowaway cultural and religious baggage from the societies they left behind, and diverse forms of generally Christian spiritual expression.

Along with Catholics and Protestants, other faiths represented, though in much smaller numbers, were Spanish Jews, Russian and Baltic Greek Orthodox (relative latecomers on the West coast), Asian Buddhists, and a plethora of animists from Africa and the American continent who believed divinity lived in all material substance. Satanic black-magic practitioners arrived from the Caribbean, plus a host of other spiritual traditions and tendencies. Even some Europeans mixed Christianity with magic and the occult.

The utter diversity of these newcomers and their eclectic spiritual habits to America almost necessitated at last nominal religious tolerance. The promiscuously varied religious and cultural distinctions of immigrants "became the foundation of diverse, historically evolving religious experience in America, both before and after the American Revolution," according to *Religion in American Life: A History*, by historians Jon Butler, Grant Wacker, and Randall Balmer.[31]

RELIGIOUS EBB AND FLOW

Scholars have long debated the ebb and flow of religious devotion in early America. But it does seem clear that it *did* ebb and flow rather than follow an undeviating trajectory of increasing piety and righteousness.

Nonetheless, religion in the colonies was culturally important from the get-go. Indeed, the original charter of the Virginia Company that established the first British New World settlement at Jamestown declared that the firm's primary goal was to Christianize native peoples it found.

Religion in American Life points out that at its debut meeting the Virginia House of Burgesses, the first colonial legislative assembly, "took up religion as a major task." The assembly commenced with a prayer and then passed laws to uphold "God's service" in the New World wilderness.[32]

"Men's affairs do little prosper where God's service is neglected," the burgesses wrote.[33]

Other colonies, such as Maryland, initially established as a Catholic enclave in 1634, also prioritized religion in civic affairs, endeavoring to "treat Protestants with as much mildness as favor and justice will permit." The stiff-necked Puritans shepherded to America in 1630 in the first large wave of immigration were initially a less tolerant lot than the Maryland papists.[34]

By Winthrop's death in Massachusetts in 1649, religious leaders in New England, Virginia and Maryland had failed to resolve strong antagonisms between Catholics and Protestants. Aggressive intolerance bloomed and with it the colonies' "early religious fervor gave way to a spiritual lethargy that lasted well into the 1680s," and church attendance deeply sagged.[35]

Religion for a time seemed to fade in importance for the offspring of early American immigrants. Boston became prosperous and worldly, and "more than half"[36] of the citizenry avoided churches. Children of Plymouth Colony settlers moved away so often in pursuit of profit and adventure that town leaders worried about the colony's survival. Even colonial clergy were seduced by greed for land.

PIETY ERODED ...

By the final decade of the seventeenth century, although religion remained foundational in New England society, second- and third-generation offspring had lost their spiritual mojo, and new immigrants from the British isles and France declined to join congregations when they arrived. Church membership that had been as high as 80 percent among early settlers plunged near century's end, with only 30 percent of taxpayers then attending regular services in Salem, Massachusetts, and only about 15 percent in the Connecticut towns of New Haven, New London, Stonington, and Woodbury.[37]

Prominent colonial clergyman Cotton Mather began to warn of increasing use of magic to cure disease, which led to increasing use of executions to dispatch witches—viewed as purveyors of "black magic"—including, famously, at Salem Village.

A number of Christian dissidents, fed up with the rigidity and hypocrisy of Puritanism, fled their communities and struck out on their own, including religious-freedom advocate Roger Williams, who founded Rhode Island Colony, and cult leader Anne Hutchinson, who was eventually killed by Indians. I will flesh out these important figures later in the book.

... AND THEN REVIVED

Religious interest in the colonies revived in the eighteenth century, driven by immigration of very spiritually diverse Europeans (including Jews and Mennonites), expansion of religious sects already present in America, and a perpetuating fascination with magic and the occult. Together, these causes "produced a religious diversity unmatched in any Old World society,"[38] according to *Religion in American Life*.

Yet, it was a mixed blessing that often proved overwhelming to unsophisticated backwoodsmen.

"Many colonists enjoyed the religious freedom that had emerged in America," the authors wrote in *Religion in American Life*. "But not everyone grappled with the confusion it produced."[39]

Still, the religious revival was manifest. Some of the qualities and practices that characterized later American "awakenings" in coming centuries were present in the 1700s, including increasing numbers of church buildings and congregations, a manic spirit of religious renewal, and the activism of women. Adding fuel to this fire of revivalism was English Anglican minister George Whitefield, who toured British colonies from 1739 to his death in 1770 in Massachusetts. His simple question to crowds reputedly as large as ten thousand people: "What must I do to be saved?"[40]

Relevant to this book, many new New England towns early in the eighteenth century embraced the region's "state-church" tradition, with churches receiving public tax funding.

This evolving culture of focused religiosity continued up to America's declaration of independence from Britain and the start of the Revolutionary

War in 1776, although the writers of the Declaration and, later, the Constitution, totally left out sectarian religion and only mentioned a deity rarely and vaguely.

During the war, military chaplains often complained of recruits marked disinterest in and even hostility toward religion, and a number of church groups suffered persecutions, including the Anglicans (Church of England), who were viewed as turncoats by colonists, and the Presbyterians, who were attacked by invading British forces in New York, Connecticut, and New Jersey.

After the war, religion revived further as citizens in victorious America believed that "a virtuous people" was necessary for the rebuilding and survival of the young democratic republic. Religion was seen as the guarantor of such virtue: "Everywhere, ministers proclaimed the fusion that came out of American independence and organized religion, especially Christianity."[41]

The number of denominations, churches and congregants then surged in the colonies. Protestant Methodism was particularly fertile, increasing its number of adherents tenfold to 150,000 during 1784 to 1810. By the 1840s, an estimated 30 to 40 percent of the overall population claimed church membership, slowly climbing to 50 percent by the beginning of the twentieth century.[42]

But the broad, Babel-like diversity of American Christianity is what bestowed its distinct character.

"Once you attempt legislation upon religious grounds, you open the way for every kind of intolerance and religious persecution."

— **William Butler Yeats** (1865–1939),
Nobel Prize-winning Irish poet and paragon
of twentieth-century literature

CHAPTER 5

INTOLERANCE

Christian sects persecute rivals

MOST PEOPLE MIGHT reasonably assume that the religious-pilgrim vibe of early America would have resulted in a generous spirit of religious tolerance. *Au contraire.*

The reformist Anglican Brownists of Plymouth Colony—later known as "Pilgrims"—who arrived on the Mayflower in 1620, as I noted previously, were certainly a kindly democratic group. Unlike the more radical separatist English Puritans who arrived in 1630.

The latter sect had sought to "purify" the Anglican Church—the official Church of England—of remnants of Catholic "popery" that clung on during the Reformation. They also wanted Puritanism nationwide to replace what they viewed as sacrilegiously ornate Anglicanism, which King Henry VIII preferred after relegating Catholicism to an inferior status in England. Puritans felt that Henry's daughter with second wife Anne Boleyn, Queen Elizabeth I, had reformed the church later as promised, albeit inadequately.

Ultimately, the Puritan campaign in England had led directly to civil war there and also helped stimulate the founding of American colonies (Puritans financed immigration voyages, as I noted earlier), and the Puritan way of life became a model for New World communities.[43]

The Puritan theocratic impulse propagated quickly and came to significantly influence other sects along America's eastern seaboard.

But once the Puritans established religious and secular control in the areas they settled in New England, a welcoming spirit of inclusivity was not their first inclination, to put it mildly. Instead, they resolutely sought, as reformist Puritan Rev. John Cotton purportedly had urged earlier, to eschew toleration and break "the very neck of Schism and vile opinions," by which they meant all *other* religious persuasions.[44] Puritans targeted spiritual tolerance as the *enemy* of American religion, not something to embrace.[45]

Thus, once established, the Puritans routinely expelled religious nonconformists from their colonies, which is exactly what happened to Roger Williams and Anne Hutchinson.

ROGER WILLIAMS

Williams (1603–1683) was a well-intentioned English Protestant theologian who had hoped to do missionary work in the New World. He arrived in Boston as a Puritan in 1631 and quickly developed a deep empathy for Native Americans. He believed colonists had no right under royal charters to arbitrarily take Indian land without Indian permission and payment. Due to this injustice, he immediately stopped preaching to indigenous people and became a sort of separatist-humanist.

Thus, he came into conflict with domineering secular and religious authorities in the town where he lived: Salem, Massachusetts (yes, *that* Salem). His heterodox attitude distressed local entrepreneurs and political leaders, who resented anyone meddling in their real-estate dreams or being "disrespectful" toward their English king's edicts. Williams also butted heads with the village's Puritan elders, who denounced him for willfully not proselytizing to the Indians, plus heresy and sedition.

Ultimately, in 1636 the Massachusetts colony banished him for "diverse, new and dangerous opinions."[46] After expulsion, he issued a passionate, principled plea for freedom of conscience in the new country that said: "God requireth not an uniformity of Religion to be inacted and enforced in any civill state; which inforced uniformity (sooner or later) is the greatest occasion of civill Warre, ravishing of conscience, persecution of Christ Jesus in his servants, and of the hypocrisie and destruction of millions of souls."[47]

When Williams was exiled, Wampanoag chief Massasoit (who had years earlier signed a treaty with the Plymouth Colony) sold him land for his new Rhode Island colony, which he founded in 1636. His guiding principle was religious freedom, because he believed "forced worship stinks in God's nostrils."[48] Williams was by then a Reformed Baptist and founder of the first Baptist church in the New World.

In a 1637 agreement in the new community, a majority vote of household heads was authorized to govern, but "only in civil things." Later in that year and again in 1640, voters re-ratified a civil-only government and freedom of conscience. The community Williams founded in Providence, Rhode Island, was the first in modern history to purposely disconnect citizenship from religion.[49]

Religious liberty in the democratic colony was legally enshrined, and church and state were irrevocably deemed separate. Williams pointed to the fact that he could find no scriptural foundation for a state church, stiffening his staunch advocacy for the separation of church and state. Furthermore, he remained a fervent champion of Indians' equality with European colonists.

Williams was a pioneer in envisioning the wisdom of church-state separation. John Dickinson, one of America's Founding Fathers, noted the virtues of this innovative political idea in 1768 as storm clouds formed ahead of the coming American Revolution:

Religion and Government are certainly very different Things, instituted for different Ends; the design of one being to promote our temporal Happiness; the design of the other to procure the Favour of God, and thereby the Salvation of our Souls. While these are kept distinct and apart, the Peace and welfare of Society is preserved, and the Ends of both are answered. By mixing them together, feuds, animosities and persecutions have been raised, which have deluged the World in Blood, and disgraced human Nature.[50]

Williams was also an innovator in diplomacy with Native Americans, and in recognizing the value of linguistics.

In his first book, *A Key Into the Language of America* (1643), Williams wrote, "Thy brother Indian is by birth as good…as wise, as fair, as strong."[51] Interestingly, the book was the first to introduce Native American languages (mainly Narragansett, an Algonquin tongue), and was the first investigation of an Amerindian language in English.

ANNE (MARBURY) HUTCHINSON

The daughter of an Anglican minister, Hutchinson (1591–1643), a Londoner, had immigrated with her husband, John, to the New World in 1633, following Puritan leader John Cotton. In the new land, she found herself dangerously isolated for upholding the minority side in a centuries-long, fundamentalist debate that continued among colonial Christians about how personal spiritual salvation could be obtained.

In this conflict, known as the Antinomian ("against the law") or "Free Grace" Controversy, Hutchinson was on the Free Grace side, espousing the "covenant of grace"—by "faith alone"—theology.[52] This view, in opposition to Puritan doctrine, held that salvation was only possible through authentic belief in Jesus Christ and not outward personal behavior or appearance of piety. Grace proponents participated in good work after they answered God's call, not to gain salvation but to demonstrate the authenticity of their calling.

As good Calvininsts, the Puritans believed, conversely, that only those specifically chosen by God for immortality—the "elect"—would be saved, not those visited by the Holy Ghost. The insecurity about who would or would not be saved among Puritans purportedly spawned an nondoctrinaire belief that God would "bless" the elect with outward signs, such as manifestations of material prosperity, personal goodness, and pronounced charitability. Hutchinson and other Anabaptists thus perhaps unfairly criticized Puritans for following the "covenant of works" they derided.

The "covenant of works" theology held that only righteous Christian behavior, or "good works," as it were, led to eternal life, and that scripture was the supreme and infallible repository of all revelation. Hutchinson, contrarily, preached that privately received revelations—i.e., visions—were as valid as those described in the Bible.

Because Hutchinson's doctrine seemed to demote the Puritans' traditional reliance on outward Christian behavior to ensure communal morality, Puritan leaders in New England grew increasingly alarmed, and then began persecuting the radical preacher.

The Controversy, which raged in the colonies from 1636 to 1638, is viewed as an important signpost in understanding the history of religion, society, and gender in colonial New England. It was as much a battle for religious supremacy as for political power.

At the heart of the divide were two wholly incompatible core ideas. Hutchinson and other reformers in Reformed, Anglican, and Lutheran sects of Protestantism held that believers received direct, new revelation continuously emanating from a personal God. The Catholic Church and conservative Protestants, such as Anabaptists, believed all revelations had ended with the Apostolic era of the twelve apostles (roughly 33–100 AD) after the death of Jesus.

Hutchinson, a midwife and mother of fifteen, eventually suffered a fate similar to Williams' at the hands of Massachusetts Bay Colony's severe Puritan establishment, which vied for control of government with other radical upstarts. She is known today as America's first female religious leader, but her strong religious convictions, personal charisma, growing popularity (with women and men) and her disconcerting *femaleness* in a patriarchal society put her at odds with the male, chauvinist, Puritan political establishment in Massachusetts.

Religious leaders feared that Hutchinson's rabble-rousing threatened a schism that would undermine Puritan power and control in the colony. Free-grace election candidates then suffered a number of electoral defeats in 1637, which emboldened the Puritan opposition and spawned accusations against Hutchinson.

At Hutchinson's trial in 1637, she claimed divine inspiration as the source of her knowledge and predicted doom for the colony. The secular court convicted her of contempt and sedition, and banished her from the colony (along with her supporters), followed the next year with excommunication by an ecclesiastic court. This carried a death sentence if she returned to the colony after exile.

Encouraged by Roger Williams, Hutchinson and many of her devotees established a settlement at Portsmouth in Rhode Island Colony, near Williams in Providence. But when her husband died a few years later and Massachusetts threatened to annex Rhode Island, Hutchinson felt compelled to move farther from the grasp of Boston. She resettled in Dutch colonial territory on Long Island Sound (near present-day Pelham Bay, New York). In 1643, Indians killed her along with all her servants and all but one of her children. Not surprisingly, some in Massachusetts believed divine justice played a role.[53]

Religious tyranny in the New World wasn't confined to the unjust experiences of Williams, Hutchinson, and other freethinkers. It was rampant throughout the colonies during their early histories.

By late in the 1600s, Puritan leaders worried that piety was fading among children and grandchildren of devout original settlers and that male church membership was declining (only men paid taxes to support the colony's official Puritan church). Consequently, rules were changed to allow more people to be baptized into the church, thus effecting greater participation in church activities (and more taxpayers). But a Christ-manifesting epiphany experience, similar to what we describe today as being "born again," was still required for full church membership.

Ultimately, Puritan power in New England ebbed as non-Puritan Christian sects and other faiths proliferated in America, and new centers of authority emerged. Even vaunted Puritan piety seemed to sag anew, and in 1769 a general synod met to consider the possible causes of the decline, blaming everything from cursing to alcohol to depravity in taverns.

In the end, the difficulty of living in a state of constant anxiety over personal salvation seemed a deciding factor. Puritans, after all, had no idea whether, even if they lived a perfect, exemplary life of total rectitude and faith, they still might end up going straight to hell.[54]

By the time the Founding Fathers went to work creating the new country, they were strongly aware of the existential dangers to it from the kind of religious tyranny and oppression the Puritans had exported to the New World.

CATHOLICS

The first Catholic émigrés had fled Protestant persecution in England. They landed in 1634 in an area just north of Virginia, where they established the Maryland Colony, situated between the Potomac River and Chesapeake Bay. The colony is commonly believed named in honor of England's Henrietta Maria, queen consort of King Charles I, although some Catholic scholars contend that it was named for the mother of Jesus.[55]

Cecil Calvert, known as Lord Baltimore, led the immigrant group. Profit was very much part of the enterprise's motivation, which rather tended to sabotage the Catholic part. Eventually, the political conflict between its discordant mixture of Catholic gentlemen and more populous Protestant laborers fractured the colony.

Trying to protect Maryland's Catholic settlers and those of other religions not aligned with the dominating Anglicanism in the colonies, Gov. William Stone in 1649 orchestrated passage by the House of Delegates of a religious-freedom law. But the Act of Toleration ensured religious liberty only for Trinitarian Christians. In 1654, a brief civil war erupted after reformist Anglican Puritans, a growing demographic in the colony, seized control of colony governance.

After the war, the act was revoked under orders of a commissioner of British Puritan leader Oliver Cromwell, and Lord Baltimore surrendered political control of Maryland. This led to Protestants replacing Catholics in the Legislature. However, the Calverts later regained control of the colony and temporarily reinstated the Christian liberty law.

Although the Act of Toleration remains an important signpost of religious freedom in the colonies and indeed ultimately led to the First Amendment in the American Bill of Rights, it was again repealed in 1692 after a 1689 Protestant rebellion in the colony. This in turn led to crown rule (1692–1715) and temporary establishment of the Church of England as the colony's official religion.[56] In 1715, the colony yet again reverted to the control of the Calvert family, which, ironically, in the interim, had become Protestant.

Of note, the act was the second legislative enactment in the American colonies to guarantee at least some religious freedom, after Roger Williams' in Rhode Island. Williams' colony, uniquely, formally codified church-state separation.

Although the Maryland colony didn't end up officially Catholic as originally intended, it was notably prosperous, aided by its most lucrative crop—tobacco—as Lord Baltimore had hoped.

Clearly, full freedom of religion did not become an actuality in the seventeenth-century colonies, with the exception of Williams' groundbreaking Rhode Island colony. Various individual colonies often established official religions, such as in New Netherland; founded in 1624, the colony in 1628 proclaimed the Dutch Reform Church as its official religion. Similarly, Virginia for a time made itself officially Anglican.

Although the US Constitution later formally codified religious freedom in America and formally separated government and faith, it did not specifically prohibit states from continuing, as they had, to publicly subsidize various religious sects.

"How could this happen here?"

— **Sir William Phips** (1651–1695),
first royal governor of Massachusetts Bay Colony
during the Salem witch trials in 1692. He ended
the trials, but only after many innocent people
already had been jailed and executed.

CHAPTER 6

SALEM'S LOT

Piety, fear unleash a wave of witch hangings

A LL SUPERSTITION, INCLUDING supernatural religion, is prone to afflicting adherents with stark terror of unseen forces. Such unreasoned fear inevitably spawns horror, as it did in this infamous chapter in colonial American history.

WITCH HUNT

Fear and shame characterized daily life in the Massachusetts Bay Colony's Puritan-governed Salem Village, where the "witch hunt" erupted from May to October 1692.

Accusations, investigations, and prosecutions were spawned by ignorance, prejudice, and religious hysteria and ultimately resulted in nineteen people being hanged (and one "prest to death") for witchcraft.[57] Many more were accused during the hysteria, leading to imprisonment of 150 suspects, the prestigious local whaling captain's wife among them. Even the wife of Massachusetts Governor William Phips was eventually among the accused.

The catastrophe began when a number of young girls, possibly fearing punishment for secular transgressions, claimed (perhaps disingenuously) that they were possessed by the devil and then made witchcraft accusations against various townspeople. The strange, infective hysteria immediately spread to many other girls in the community.

Salem was ripe for such a social cataclysm. Seventeenth-century colonists shared a belief in supernatural beings and that Satan was active on Earth, an evil fantasy that was the fundamental viral agent of this sordid episode.

Salem Village was a rigid Calvinist Puritan place, where music, dancing, and celebration of holidays including Christmas and Easter were banned, along with toys and especially dolls (considered idolatrous and potentially satanic). Citizens were required to attend three-hour sermons twice weekly; local civic life revolved around the church meeting house, and children learned to abjectly fear eternal damnation.[58]

The catastrophe in Salem was just one event in a continuing plague of witch-hunt debacles that were spawned in Western Europe between 1300 and 1330, and continued until late in the eighteenth century (a final witchcraft execution was conducted in Switzerland in 1782). The historical consensus is that more than one hundred thousand people were tried for witchcraft during this appalling period in the late Middle Ages, and between forty thousand to sixty thousand alleged witches were ultimately executed.[59]

Rather than chasing down *known* witches, the so-called "hunts" sought to identify secret witches living amongst the faithful. Christians in that day believed witches exchanged their souls with Satan for superpowers, including being able to transform from human to animal and back again. Witches purportedly flew to clandestine night meetings and orgies, and planned dastardly, soul-destroying deeds.

The emergence of chauvinistic witch hysteria in the late Middle Ages likely was partly a response to major cultural changes in Europe at the time. Witchcraft imagery scholar Charles Zika, a professor at University of Melbourne, Australia, has written:

> *It's bound up with an anxiety about women and what place they have in society at a time when Europe was undergoing fundamental changes and transformations in society.... It seems to me that this idea of them flying out the chimney is actually kind of a protest against this*

confinement in domestic space. Witchcraft is symbolically in some ways
freeing individuals from that kind of conception of their realm.[60]

The effects of this viral irrational fear of female freedom and promiscuity during the Protestant Reformation upheavals included the compulsion of some religious leaders to prohibit alcohol and dancing, to close brothels, and to enforce stricter rules controlling marriage.

Executions were the culmination of an escalating continuum of private suspicion, rampant public rumor, arrest, trial, and conviction. Virtually any accusation of witchcraft was reportedly treated with utmost terror and seriousness by most people in the seventeenth-century colonies. The Salem tragedy was the culmination during the seventeenth century of a lethal stew of prepubescent hysteria, internecine religious squabbles, local politics, family animosities, and unnerving religious fear. It even began to spread to other communities.

The Salem girls' increasingly bizarre behavior, including shrieks, fits, and vomiting, have been credited to an assortment of speculative causes, including the influence of a local Voodoo-believing servant woman named Tituba, disease, and ingestion of bread infected with the local fungus ergot, of which LSD is a derivative. In any event, the behavior deeply alarmed the devil-obsessed populace. Initially, two girls—Betty Williams, nine, and sister Abigail, eleven—accused Tituba, a Salem household slave woman from Barbados, whose ethnicity is still unconfirmed.

Under extreme duress in her prosecution, Tituba finally ignited the proceedings with a "psychedelic confession" in which she admitted conferring with the devil, and she also fingered eight locals as fellow witches, including some community stalwarts.[61] Eventually, dozens of the accused proved to be known enemies of a grasping, social-climbing local family, the Putnams. Many Salem citizens who began to see the accusations and trials as a travesty held their tongues, worried they might be next hauled to the dock in the general hysteria. The trials began on May 27, and the first hanging was June 10. On July 19, five more were hanged, five others on August 19, the final eight on September 22.

Acute witch-hunt hysteria started to calm by the end of September in Salem and environs. Public opinion turned against the accusers, the general craziness, and the trials being conducted in various towns in Massachusetts Bay Colony. Gov. Phips, furious over accusations against his wife, dismantled the court in October. He immediately pardoned the condemned who were still alive and released remaining prisoners.

The colony's legislature later rescinded the trials' convictions and paid reparations to families of those executed. In a 1693 letter, the governor lamented the period of frenzied depravity as a "blak cloud that threatened this Province with destruccion."[62]

MORE HORROR

Salem's eruption wasn't an isolated event just in Massachusetts. Twelve other people had been previously executed for witchcraft throughout New England from 1647 to 1688.[63]

Magic in the gothic world Hawthorne wrote about was not pulling rabbits out of hats. Rather, it was the "double, double toil and trouble/fire burn, and caldron bubble" of the fearsome, witchy hags in Shakespeare's *Macbeth*. As Voltaire bemoaned, "superstition is, after the plague, the most horrible flail that can infect mankind.... The church has always condemned magic but has always believed in it. Magic rose in the East and then became enshrined in Christianity."[64]

So, for much of the second half of the seventeenth century, colonial Americans frequently appeared to be ruled not, in Abraham Lincoln's elegant phrase, by "the better angels of our nature," but the worst. As were people elsewhere, including Europe, where thousands of alleged witches were also executed.

American colonists were Europeans first, after all.

"The voice of the Great Spirit is heard in the twittering of birds, the rippling of mighty waters, and the sweet breathing of flowers. If this is Paganism, then at present, at least, I am a Pagan."

— **Zitkala Sa (a.k.a. Red Bird)** (1876–1938), female Sioux leader, writer, and musician

CHAPTER 7

THE GREAT SPIRIT

*American colonists encounter rich
indigenous religious traditions*

WHEN DEVOUT EUROPEAN Christians began arriving in the New World, they discovered that the people already there had long worshipped their own God and embraced an alien sense of the sacred, one that could be physically touched.

Stones radiated divinity. Hallucinations had concrete meaning.

The newcomers brought with them the Christian beliefs of a supernatural deity and unreachable invisible realms where the spirits of their faith resided. Native Americans, on the other hand, were largely *animist*, believing that a divine spirit directly animates everything in the phenomenal universe.

To native Americans, mountains, streams, and forests embody the *Great Spirit*, which is to say, God. In indigenous "religion," Many Indians found the term "religion" inappropriate to their traditional tribal belief systems, which they viewed as simply common-sense acknowledgements of reality. Indian faiths generally assume that human beings and spirits are able to move fluidly back and forth between physical and sacred worlds—as when instructive phantasms emanate from self-inflicted hardship or drug-induced "vision quests."

RELIGIONS OF KINDNESS, GENEROSITY

Native Americans, then as now, commonly view spirituality not as ritual and dogma but as the apparent relationships among and between people and other entities, including nature, ancestors and people as yet unborn, as well as imagined beings and sacred objects. They don't generally argue about religious ideas; they live them as a natural part of existence.

But, of course, it isn't that simple. At the time of America's early colonization, some three hundred different languages in thirty to fifty identified linguistic groups were extant among hundreds of indigenous tribes, and, despite similarities, spiritual traditions were localized and diverse.

Some tribes, like those in the powerful Iroquois confederacy in New England, envisioned a single supreme creator who gave original instructions to humans, similar to then-current Christian doctrine. But others, such as the Alaskan Koyukon, were in thrall to a variety of sacred entities, such as the Raven, mirroring many pre-Christian pagan belief systems.

Even so, some native spiritual traditions are broadly shared. In Wyoming, a nearly 1,300-foot-tall monolith called Devil's Tower (a.k.a. Bear Lodge Butte) embodies several versions of the creation myths of various tribes, including the Lakota Sioux and Kiowa peoples, and has spiritual connections to some twenty different indigenous groups.

In one version, the distinct vertical striations on the sides of the conical outcropping are believed to have been created by bears chasing three little girls to the top of the rock, where they prayed to the Great Spirit to save them. The Great Spirit caused the rock to grow toward the heavens to prevent the bears from reaching their prey, and the clawing, grasping bears purportedly left deep gouges still strikingly visible today. Once the girls touched the sky, they turned into stars.

Another version of the story involves two boys and one huge bear—but the bear leaves in frustration and goes to yet another landmark, Bear Butte in South Dakota, now a sacred Lakota site. Indeed, the Sioux consider South Dakota's entire sprawling Black Hills region, which encompasses Bear Butte, to be sacred even though the US government long ago annexed it in patently dishonest treaties.

Fundamentally, Native American spirituality values communal

participation over dogma, interpersonal kindness and generosity over doctrinaire ritual. Spreading happiness and calm, and honoring nature are spiritual acts among Indian religious traditions, making them simultaneously primitive and contemporary. Primitive in that the nurturing of relationships has been essential to most kinship groups throughout history; contemporary in that honoring nature has become a core doctrine of modern environmentalism.

Interestingly, the Indian view of creation is decidedly local compared to its more universal quality in Christian scripture's Genesis account. For Indians, creation is generally believed to have occurred in the vicinity of where they live, so that particular local landmarks involved in their creation myths acquire deeply sacred status.

ATTITUDES TOWARD DEATH

Native American beliefs and attitudes toward death are somewhat diverse and complex. Some traditions hold that spirits or essences of the deceased can linger and cause trouble for the living. Others view the dead with great reverence and respect—*and* wariness.

A visual cliché in American movies about the old West are Indian "graveyards" with the dead lying on raised scaffolding adorned with feathers, beads, and other honoring items. Mounted cowboys or soldiers unexpectedly coming upon such a place always back away, quietly, slowly, pointedly avoiding it, sensing the spiritual power of the burial realm as viscerally terrifying.

Unfortunately, the arrival of Europeans proved catastrophic not only for Native American people but also their spiritual traditions. When the Pilgrims landed in 1620, many villages were already deserted as disease brought by earlier white adventurers had wiped out thousands of native people. Because Native Americans had no written languages, their collective knowledge also died when disease or warfare with whites mowed down tribes. Without written records, much indigenous knowledge, traditionally handed down orally through generations, disappeared.

Today, native tribes have begun trying to resurrect still-extant but long-dormant traditional cultures and languages before they disappear entirely.

THE GHOST DANCE

Ironically, Native Americans' tendency to incorporate Christian beliefs into their indigenous faiths helped deliver the final, fatal *coup d'état* to traditional Indian culture in America.

A desperate Indian spiritual movement on the Great Plains late in the nineteenth century synthesized indigenous and Christian beliefs in a charismatic doctrine that envisioned a throwing off of white oppression and a rebirth of traditional Indian self-sufficiency.

Over time the white government had pushed Indians off their lands onto reservations, dislocating them from their traditional ways of life, stimulating a couple of similar mystical movements around two holy men. These movements arose in in the late 1800s in response to deep resentment and anxiety among indigenous people.

The movements, ironically, envisioned a Christianity-inspired imminent return of the dead (the "ghosts"), who would expel whites and restore Indian traditional life amid plenty (Indian people were by then already being influenced by the European faith). Adherents believed that special songs and dances as well as following a strict moral code resembling Christianity would usher in all Indians' salvation and, importantly, bring back the huge buffalo herds that had disappeared from the landscape. Also, of particular concern to the white-government military, Indian dancers believed bullets could not penetrate their sacred "ghost shirts."

Two Indian prophets—Wodziwob and Wovoka—embodied these closely related spiritual movements. Wodziwob (Gray Hair), of the Northern Paiute tribe in what is now Nevada, was the first, starting his preaching on Walter Lake Reservation in 1870. He told of a trance he experienced where he traveled to a supernatural realm and was informed there how Indians could create a new paradise with sacred rituals. The so-called Ghost Dance movement (the dance was a central ritual) gradually petered out after Wodziwob's prophesy did not materialize and he died. But another Paiute medicine man, Wovoka, had participated in the Ghost Dance of 1870 and would bring it back to life.

While ill in late 1888, Wovoka envisioned a new Ghost Dance, and during a solar eclipse on January 1, 1889, he had what he believed was a sacred epiphany. In this vision, he was transported to the spirit world and saw all his dead ancestors, again alive, and saw all Indians rising into the sky. He envisioned all remaining whites being sucked into the earth, and all Indians—joined by returning ancestors—gathering to enjoy a revitalized life on earth free of aliens. Wovoka had been taught by Presbyterians in his youth, and he reportedly used self-inflicted *stigmata* wounds on his hands and feet to inspire belief that he was a new Jesus, a Messiah for the Indian people.[65]

Ironically, Wovoka stressed that peaceful, upright behavior was the path to salvation, and he urged nonviolence. Cooperation with the whites, he preached, would ensure Indian equality with them in the next life.

Tragically but perhaps inevitably, such charismatic movements spooked rather than assured the US government, prompting it to dispatch military force for a final major Indian-crushing campaign a few years after the first Ghost Dance movement emerged in 1870. This war-footing led to the infamous June 1876 massacre of General George Armstrong Custer's roughly 210-man 7th Cavalry battalion by several thousand Lakota, Northern Cheyenne, and Arapaho warriors gathered in an enormous encampment near the Little Bighorn River in Montana Territory. The engagement, commonly referred to as "Custer's Last Stand," by whites, was known by Indians as the "Battle of the Greasy Grass," after the waterway's indigenous name.

Yet the Indian victory over Custer proved fleeting, quickly resulting in indigenous calamity. In truth, it was the Indians' last stand, not Custer's. Stunned and outraged by the massacre, The US Army methodically destroyed Native American power to resist over the next few years. The relentless military campaign ended with an army massacre of hundreds of men, women, and children in December 1890 at Wounded Knee in what is now South Dakota.

MODERN INDIAN SPIRITUALITY

American Indian Christian communities of various spiritual complexions—a modern hybrid, the Native American Church (NAC), interweaves Christian and Indian spiritual ideas—still exist in the US today. The NAC also incorporates an added punch: a hallucinogenic cactus "button" called peyote, whose mescaline properties trigger phantasms seen as sacred revelations, thus retaining at least one ancient practice of their religion.

Even the US Supreme Court ultimately ruled to protect that practice as religious. It had been a long road.

From the Wounded Knee Massacre to the 1960s, according to Vine Deloria Jr.'s *God Is Red: A Native View of Religion*,[66] Indians became "Vanishing Americans," as most other Americans assumed a majority of tribes had been eradicated in warfare in the previous century. American Indian groups continued to be discriminated against, cheated, and neglected by the government, including in protecting their religious-freedom rights.

POLITICAL GAINS

Prominent Indian protests over a number of years started in 1968 when a group of Akwesasne Mohawks blockaded the Canadian crossing at Cornwall Bridge over an alleged treaty violation. The Akwesasne Reserve straddles the International Seaway Bridge area between Massena, New York, in the US, and Cornwall, Ontario, Canada. The Indian protesters correctly assert that the Jay Treaty of 1794 allowing unobstructed Indian crossings of the bridge had been violated by Canadian authorities, and they were later acquitted after fifty protesters were arrested.

That widely publicized protest is believed to have spawned a number of other Indian protests across the US in the next few years as a young generation of Indians sought to claim their constitutional and legal rights, including religious rights.

The American Indian Religious Freedom Act (AIRFA),[67] passed in 1978, affirmed and codified Indian's civil liberties, and their complete religious and cultural freedom of expression and exercise, including having practicable access to sacred sites. The act also formally acknowledged prior interference by government agencies in Indian religious practices, and required its immediate elimination.

According to Deloria in *God Is Red*, from 1972 to 1990 two major phenomena occurred: Many churches began attempting to meld traditional Christianity with Native American religious ideology, and non-Indians developed an intense if sometimes trivializing interest in Indian life and its religious beliefs and practices. Simultaneously, some groups of Indians began to return to traditional indigenous ways of life and belief.

Through it all, Deloria contends that Indians generally maintained their spiritual focus on the primacy of nature, and on nurturing positive relationships among living beings in the world.

Meanwhile, Indians today continue to struggle against marginalization and discrimination in American society, despite some noteworthy successes, such as AIRFA.

"Slaves, accept the authority of your masters with all deference, not only those who are kind and gentle but also those who are harsh.... If you endure when you are beaten for doing wrong, what credit is that? But if you endure when you do right and suffer for it, you have God's approval."

— 1 Peter 2:18–29

CHAPTER 8

NEGRO SPIRITUAL

Slaves evolve a faith of their own

PERHAPS SURPRISINGLY FROM a modern perspective, many plantation slave owners in the antebellum American South aggressively—if unsuccessfully—opposed their chattel, their property, being Christianized.

Slave owners feared the potentially liberating, radicalizing effect that finding Jesus might have on their unsophisticated field slaves. But whatever heavy obstacles to worship that their masters threw on the path to redemption, eventually including laws that legally separated them from Christian faith, slaves found a way to Christianity, some developing a rich, uniquely African-American Christian culture characterized by mystical, joyous abandon.

God and Jesus were everywhere in America before the Civil War, and slaves had little trouble finding them.

Unfortunately and hypocritically, many if not most of the pious emigrant European Christians populating the new country did little or nothing to stop the horrendous and growing practice of slavery in its various forms in colonial America. Nonetheless, not all Christians were complicit in the perpetuation of slavery in the new land; a not insignificant number viscerally opposed it. Yet the realities of bondage resulted in a new spiritual innovation being born to the American faith—black Christianity—which eventually also would significantly expand the overall Christian footprint in New World.

Indeed, Christian churches today with predominantly African American congregations define many black communities in the United States and provide critical sources of local social unity and positive political organization. The urgent pulse of those early years of hybrid, *creolized* negro Christianity can still be clearly felt in the joyful, charismatic cadences of contemporary African American church services.

Blacks today comprise about 6.7 percent of American Christians, according to a 2017 report by Pew Research Center. Major black churches include Baptist, Methodist, Pentecostal, Holiness, and Nondenominational congregations. Unsurprisingly, they predominate in Southern former slave states along the Mexican Gulf and Atlantic Ocean.[68]

AN AGRICULTURAL EDEN

Slavery flourished in America because the new country proved to be an agricultural paradise. The economics of colonies' labor-intensive plantations required armies of cheap laborers to plant, harvest, and process the enormous quantities of cotton, sugar cane, tobacco, and other cash crops the planters produced. Enter African slaves.

In the first paragraph of the introduction to his anthology, *Proslavery and Sectional Thought in the Early South: 1740–1829*, editor Jeffrey Robert Young explained how ruthlessly soulless American slavery was:

> *Over the course of four centuries, slavery in the New World generated immense profit and political power for European investors and American masters at an almost inconceivable expense in human suffering.... white and African entrepreneurs transported more than eleven million African slaves to plantations and mines in the western hemisphere. From its inception to its demise, this grotesque system of coerced labor existed as a means toward financial gain.[69]*

The first African laborers in America, a group of about nineteen, reportedly arrived in Jamestown, Virginia in 1620, brought by Dutch traders who had acquired them from a captured Spanish ship (they were likely indentured, not enslaved, in pre-slavery Jamestown). But by the time America declared its independence in 1776, slavery was legal in all thirteen colonies. Several years later, however, some colonies began one by one to outlaw the practice as an abolitionist impulse took root.

Nevertheless, in the 1800s slavery was at its height with more than four million enslaved blacks in America, most of them on Southern plantations. It took until 1863 during the Civil War for slavery to become universally outlawed with President Lincoln's Emancipation Proclamation, later formally ratified by Congress' Thirteenth Amendment in 1865.

Interestingly, one of the precursors of America's Revolutionary War against Britain had been a British court decision—*Somerset vs. Stewart*, 1772—which ordered the release of an African-English slave from bondage. The decision, effectively banning slavery *within* Britain, hinged on the rationale that "chattel slavery" was not supported by common law in England and Wales. This unprecedented decision seemed ominously foreboding to Southern American slaveholders, who were also facing growing opposition from Northern abolitionists in their own country. They worried that unchecked abolitionist fervor could ultimately destroy their wealth-producing livelihoods.

In 1808 the British parliament passed the Slave Trade Act, which prohibited new slave commerce over the Atlantic Ocean but did not outlaw slavery where it already existed in its colonies, and did not impact newly independent America. The Slavery Abolition Act of 1833 was more comprehensive, but not until 1843 would Britain completely outlaw slavery and its trade throughout the British Empire.

American slaveholders, with trepidation but not inertia, read the writing on the wall. Slave masters quickly responded with a public relations program, propagating ostensibly scriptural, legal, and political justifications for slavery. They also appropriated as much temporal power as possible to enforce the South's economic status quo. Keep in mind that most presidents preceding Lincoln were pro-slavery Southerners.

THE BIBLE SAYS SO

One factor that seemed to give slavery a rationale in the antebellum New World and elsewhere was the widely accepted idea that it was biblically ordained, as the quotation opening this chapter underscores.

Indeed, the Bible portrays slaves as human property whose lives, if not inconsequential (they had economic value and some personal protection codified in scripture), are of lesser importance than free persons, and scripture even condones masters' execution of slaves for prescribed serious offenses, but not murder. Whereas Judaic and Christian scriptural injunctions prescribe the death penalty for beating a free man to death, the same offense committed against a slave only carried a death penalty if the injured slave did not survive "for one or two days" after the assault. More modern versions of the Bible translate the "one or two days" passage as implying recovery, not lingering misery before dying.[70]

In one of the most famous early American religious sermons, *A Model of Christian Charity* (1630), Puritan layman and leader John Winthrop assured the faithful that God himself approved of slavery because the Bible says "in all times some must be rich, some poor, some high and eminent in power and dignity; others mean and in subjection."

Another Christian scripture implicitly authorizes slavery by not admonishing slaveholders to free their slaves but only to treat them with kindness and fairness. Saint Paul explicitly admonished slaves to "obey their masters." But colonial bigots commandeered and purposefully misrepresented scripture to teach the faithful not only to hold African slaves in particular contempt but to believe it had biblical endorsement.

Clerics, quoting Genesis, arbitrarily contended that Africans descended from Ham, the accursed son of Noah, although there is no language in scripture that supports that view.[71] "In time, the connection Europeans made between sin, slavery, skin colour and beliefs would condemn Africans," a 2007 BBC article pointed out.[72]

In fact, the entire section in Genesis that presents Noah's supposed accursing of Canaan, the son of Noah's youngest son, Ham, is replete with confusion and incoherence. The gist of the story is that Ham found his father drunk and naked one night, and then, asking his brothers for help, covered him. Scripture says Noah became enraged when he awoke and discovered what Ham had done, but it makes no sense that the patriarch would then curse Canaan—sentencing him to a life of servitude—rather than Ham, the actual perpetrator. Also it is not clear what Ham's actual offense was.

Whatever the self-serving interpretations of this ancient tale, some antebellum Southern intellectuals in America popularized the invented idea that black people were descendants of Ham and, like Canaan, divinely intended forever to be in servitude, and also that superior white people descended from Noah's son Shem.

These arbitrary racial ideas greatly encouraged and assisted the ideology of mainly Christian slaveowners from medieval to antebellum times. Biblical cover effectively immunized them against guilt about nurturing an immoral system.

But, there were complications.

British Anglican canon law in colonial times, for example, legally required that *baptized* slaves be freed. This led to rampant apprehension among American slaveholders that prompted passage of six colonial laws in the early 1700s codifying that slave owners were not legally obliged to free their baptized slaves. Major churches in the south were split concerning the matter of slavery, but it was Christian denominations in England and elsewhere in America, particularly Quakers, that eventually became the loudest voices against the practice.

Another biased attitude among slaveholders was the idea that Christian slaves were somehow *worse* slaves because faith gave them potentially subversive ideas—e.g., "tear to pieces the ropes of the yoke...let the oppressed go free." (Isaiah 58:6)

Christianity's stated virtues ironically served to spotlight for slaves the appalling injustices they endured at the hands of their purportedly religious masters. The unwelcome juxtaposition of these likewise made slave owners wary of the unintended effects on their charges of any formal religious instruction.

In 1723, an apparently literate mulatto slave in Virginia who had been "baptized and brought up in the Christian faith" wrote a mournful, unsigned letter to the Protestant bishop of London, describing the brutalities of masters against slaves in the New World. The writer protested that masters treated slaves like dogs, marooned "in ignorance of salvation…kept out of the church, and matrimony is denied us." Despite mortal fear of "going near to swing on the gallows tree" should his master learn of the letter, the slave wrote it anyway, pleading for "release…out of this cruel bondage."[73] The letter vanished in London's church bureaucracy and was lost to history until historians discovered it in the 1990s.

The lost letter is an apt metaphor for the widespread official indifference to slavery's moral implications during the colonial period. One slave once noted the appalling duplicity when a slave owner cum preacher served a slave Communion in the morning and then whipped him when he returned a few minutes late to the plantation that afternoon.[74]

Indeed, slavery was generally seen by the free as so utterly normal that slave owners had a term for an overwhelming desire of a slave to escape: *drapetania*. It was viewed as an inexplicably deviant impulse.[75]

SLAVE RELIGION

Even as late as the 1800s, slaves were commonly prohibited from worshipping on their plantations, thus forcing them to meet in secret in swamps and other rural hideaways, far from overseer patrols, although academics still debate how frequently slaves generally worshipped.

After the so-called "Gabrielle's Revolt," an abortive slave uprising planned on August 30, 1800 (betrayal from within and torrential rains precluded it), some slave owners felt safer allowing slaves to openly worship on plantations, where they could keep an eye on them. Some slaves were thus encouraged to worship at "home" or in white churches for surveillance. Nonetheless, the failed revolt caused planters to greater tighten restrictions on slaves otherwise to control what information they might be exposed to. Gabrielle was literate and his extra mobility due to blacksmithing jobs led him to learn about previous revolts elsewhere and possible domestic and foreign support from whites, as well as "freedom" as a political ideal.

Although punishments for violators often included whippings at plantations where slave worship was banned, some slaves still reportedly persisted in sneaking away to hold prayer meetings. Peter Randolph, enslaved in Prince

George County, Virginia, until he was freed in 1847, said of the clandestine worship meetings, "The slave forgets all his sufferings, except to remind others of the trials during the past week, exclaiming, 'Thank God, I shall not live here always!'"[76]

The faith of slaves often incorporated traditional African religious practices they brought with them on the Atlantic passage. These were also sometimes hybridized from a style of Christianity previously imposed on their communities in Africa by colonial European evangelists or in earlier enslavement on Caribbean islands.

The close proximity of slaves located on contiguous plantations encouraged personal interaction and the evolution of a unique slave culture and shared beliefs, including religious ones. This enhanced their Americanization "while simultaneously fostering retention of much of their Africanity," wrote Colin A. Palmer in *Passageways: An Interpretive History of Black America.*[77]

In the mix were traditional African spiritual beliefs and practices. Some scholars believe the African influence was more pronounced among slaves in the Caribbean, where plantations were often closer together and slaves more numerous in each than on the mainland, and education was more limited so their indigenous cultural practices were more robustly maintained. But it also reportedly occurred among African American slaves. Historian Albert J. Raboteau wrote that "even as the gods of Africa gave way to the God of Christianity, the African heritage of singing, dancing, spirit possession, and magic continued to influence Afro-American spirituals, ring shouts, and folk beliefs."[78]

American slaves also, reasonably, found American cultural practices jarringly contrary to the moral teachings of Christianity that the nation seemed to so fully embrace. Frederick Douglass, an escaped slave who became a noted abolitionist social reformer and writer, once described the chasm between pure Christianity and how it was practiced in the South as "so wide, that to receive the one as good, pure, and holy, is of necessity to reject the other as bad, corrupt, and wicked."[79]

After the Civil War, 136 religious and secular songs of African American slaves were collected by white northerners and published as *Slave Songs of the United States.* Some of the lyrics were written with code words about their desire for freedom (so if slave owners read them their meaning would be opaque).[80]

REVIVAL!

Despite some efforts to thwart it, slaves' attraction to Christianity continued to grow, especially during several waves of evangelical Protestant revivalism, termed "Awakenings," that swept over the country from the early eighteenth to late nineteenth centuries.

Christianized slaves, generally illiterate and with a primitive grasp of English, often had trouble understanding the formal, stilted liturgy in Anglican services. But they were captivated by the Awakenings' plain-speaking Methodist and Baptist firebrands. The revivalists' approach was to stress the visceral, mystic *experience* of Christian rebirth—described by Maryland slave John Thompson as "glad tidings to poor bondsmen."[81]

Revival fever spread from plantation to plantation in Thompson's area during an Awakening in the early 1800s, attracting nearly all of the slaves in the area. These revivalist eruptions were when black Christianity really seemed to take off. Data indicates that the number of black Methodists in the United States grew from about 3,800 in 1786 to nearly thirty-two thousand by 1809, and membership in black Baptist congregations jumped from 18,000 in 1793 to forty thousand in 1813.[82] Thereafter, the population of Southern black Christians exploded, increasing to five hundred thousand by the eve of the Civil War. (See Chapter 11 for details about the Awakenings.)

Slave conspiracies in 1822 and 1831 further alarmed masters. The first, planned but never executed, was led by Denmark Vesey, a former slave who had gained his freedom in South Carolina. The second, however, turned into a famous and bloody revolt led by the charismatic slave-preacher Nat Turner in Virginia. Vesey and Turner both reportedly believed God had instructed them to attack whites, further reinforcing the white bias that Christianizing slaves was a very bad idea, indeed.

A video available on YouTube, "Nat Turner: A Troublesome Property," analyzes different interpretations of Turner's uprising and its historical importance.[83] Turner's uprising was the most horrific—fifty-one white men, women, and children were murdered. White authorities eventually captured all the black insurrectionists, executing fifty-six of them, while another two hundred slaves were "beaten by angry mobs or white militias."[84]

The revolts also prompted local authorities to ban for a time black gatherings of any kind for any reason. Some authorities decreed that a white preacher had to attend every black service. Nonetheless, southern slave owners, stung by mounting abolitionist pressure from the north, thereafter slowly began to encourage conversion of slaves in hopes of deflecting criticism.

JESUS THE LIBERATOR

Negro slaves in nineteenth-century America had a different view of Christianity, Jesus, and "the promised land" than did white congregants.

Historians note that antebellum African Americans in the South viewed Jesus as a prophet of the poor and suffering, not the high and mighty. They believed that America, not Jerusalem, was their promised land, where justice and freedom would one day lead to their final liberation from bondage.

At heart, antebellum Negro faith was about justice. As former slave Jane Simpson once recalled, "I used to hear old slaves pray and ask God when would de bottom rail be de top rail, and I wondered what on earth, dey talkin' about. Dey was talkin' about when dey goin' to get from under bondage. 'Course I know now."[85]

PART II

EXPANSION, EMBEDDING

"During almost fifteen centuries has the legal establishment of Christianity been on trial. What has been its fruits? More or less, in all places, pride and indolence in the clergy; ignorance and servility in the laity; in both, superstition, bigotry and persecution."

— **James Madison** (1751–1836), American founding father, fourth president of the United States, and the recognized "founder of the Constitution"

CHAPTER 9

OUR WARY FOUNDERS

Religious freedom for all; dominance for none

R ELIGIOUS FREEDOM AND tolerance were hardly extant foundational principles of prototype America for the early colonists.

While mostly Protestant sects spread and established separate colonies, church leaders generally insisted on strict religious homogeneity in their own locales and were intolerant of alien creeds. Scattered sects did not tend to intermingle; therefore, particular denominations often became *de facto* official religions of individual colonies and, later, states.

When the US Constitution was approved in 1787 at the Constitutional Convention in Philadelphia, Article VI specified that "no religious Test shall ever be required as a Qualification to any Office or public Trust under the United States." The First Amendment, signed in 1791, prescribed religious liberty for all. Also, the Constitution's lack of direct reference to a personal God and the enshrinement of religious liberty in the First Amendment further underlined the founders' intent that the United States be a secular republic, not a theocracy, under any faith.

This led Declaration of Independence author and US Constitution participant Thomas Jefferson and his confederates to seek similar laws in his home state, Virginia. The Virginia Act for Establishing Religious Freedom signed in 1786—the year before the Constitution was signed—codified full religious freedom for that state what the Constitution would later mandate for the federal government.

Although Anglicans were the majority and their church had long been Virginia's official faith by 1786, other sects in the colony were growing fast (particularly Baptists, Presbyterians, and Methodists), and were chafing under the taxes and dominion of Anglicans.

Jefferson stressed that the new Virginia religious freedom law was not just ecumenical but encompassed all faiths (as well as no faith). He wrote that it was "meant to comprehend, within the mantle of its protection, the Jew, the Gentile, the Christian and the Mahometan, the Hindoo and Infidel of every denomination."

In endorsing such freedom, Jefferson memorably argued that "it does me no injury for my neighbor to say there are twenty gods or no God. It neither picks my pocket nor breaks my leg."

The Virginia Anglicans were the second most dominant sect in early America (after New England Congregationalists), adopting Europe's ancient church-state collaborative model of governance. Virginia was the largest colony in area and the most populous—up to US independence its extent encompassed or claimed what would become the modern states of West Virginia, Kentucky, Indiana, and Illinois, and parts of Ohio and Western Pennsylvania.

Colonial Virginia's first elected assembly, the House of Burgesses, established the Anglican faith as the colony's official religion in 1632. Religious laws it passed mandated "uniformitie throughout the colony both in substance and circumstance to the cannons and constitution of the Church of England."[86] Only Anglicans could hold public office. Strange as it seems now in a modern American context, laymen then working for the Virginia church even received and dispersed local taxes for civic needs, such as road building and poor relief.[87]

Despite the broad authority of colonial Virginian Anglicanism, dissident religious groups still proliferated throughout the colony, especially in remote rural areas, and they grew at a faster clip than the mainstream faith. Eventually, religious conflict became political dynamite in the colony. Anglican taxes were the fuse.

Virginia planter George Mason, a delegate to America's first Constitutional Convention, stipulated in Virginia's 1776 Declaration of Rights that no citizen "should be compelled to contribute to the maintenance of a church with which their consciences will not permit them to join, and from which they can derive no benefit... and that equal liberty as well religious as civil, may be universally extended to all the good people of this commonwealth."

However, even though non-members could now opt out of its taxes, the Church of England remained Virginia's official church for another decade.

THE DEIST FOUNDERS

As Jefferson did, many of the Founding Fathers viewed such early theocratic tendencies in America as a clear and present danger to the new republic. However, as men of their times they also generally if somewhat uneasily understood that religion, specifically Christianity, offered civilizing and stabilizing virtues.

But politically they well understood the catastrophic, destabilizing effects throughout Europe, then still occurring, of religious hegemony and imperialism, and the resulting warfare and injustice.

Equally opposed to religious tyranny was another Virginia planter and our fourth president, James Madison, a key drafter and promoter of the US Constitution and Bill of Rights. Among his stated reasons for why the state should not support publicly financed Christian instruction, he wrote, "the Religion then of every man must be left to the conviction and conscience of every... man to exercise it as these may dictate. This right is in its nature an inalienable right." Madison also warned that government endorsement of any particular religion threatened all religion, because it could easily lead to "exclusion of all other sects." He remembered heterodox Baptist ministers previously arrested by Anglican authorities in Virginia.

Many founders weren't mainstream Christians but Enlightenment-style Deists who believed not in a personal deity but in a remote, impersonal creator God. The deity of Deists spun existence in motion and then virtually disappeared to let the created but self-governing forces of the universe do what they naturally would.

America's second president, John Adams, held antagonistic sentiments toward coercive faith similar to Madison's. "This is my religion... joy and exaltation in my own existence... so go ahead and snarl... bite... howl, you Calvinistic divines and all you who say I am no Christian. I say you are not Christian."[88] In an 1825 letter to Jefferson, a rival and longtime friend, Adams lamented colonial statutes drafted to punish skeptics of the Bible. Such laws, he wrote, are "a great embarrassment, great obstructions to the improvement of the human mind. Books that cannot bear examination certainly ought not to be established as divine inspiration by penal laws."[89]

Jefferson himself was strictly a materialist. "To talk of immaterial existences is to talk of nothings," Jefferson wrote in a letter to John Adams dated August 15, 1820, reflecting Deists' philosophical unease with supernatural ideas that ignore the need for verifiability. "To say that the human soul, angels, god, are immaterial, is to say they are nothings, or that there is no god, no angels, no soul.... At what age of the Christian church this heresy of immaterialism, this masked atheism, crept in, I do not know. But heresy it certainly is."[90] Jefferson made it clear that, to him, worshipping phantasms was heresy.

But few of the founders were as strident regarding the precepts of Christianity as influential colonial agitator Thomas Paine (1737–1809), who viewed the faith as absurdly inconsistent with reality. In his radical *The Age of Reason*, he wrote that "there is none more derogatory to the Almighty, more unedifying to man, more repugnant to reason, and more contradictory in itself than this thing called Christianity." He believed the faith arbitrarily empowered and enriched clergy and led the faithful nowhere useful.

First American President George Washington joined Adams, Jefferson, and Madison among founders zealously opposing religious tyranny of any kind in America.

In a 1790 letter to leaders of the country's oldest synagogue in Newport, Rhode Island, Washington promised Jewish congregants complete religious autonomy. "All possess alike liberty of conscience and immunity of citizenship," he wrote to the Touro Synagogue. "For happily the Government of the United States, which gives to bigotry no sanction, to persecution no assistance requires only that they who live under its protection should demean themselves as good citizens."

In a 1793 letter to the New Church in Baltimore, Maryland, Washington expressed his Enlightenment materialist sensibilities. He stressed that in America "the light of truth and reason has triumphed over the power of bigotry and superstition," and that all citizens were entitled to worship as they wished without fear or opposition.[91]

NOT CHRISTIAN 'IN ANY SENSE'

Also of note, Amendment XI of the 1797 peace and friendship Treaty of Tripoli, written by Adams and approved by Washington, noted that "the Government of the United States of America is not, in any sense, founded on the Christian religion."[92]

Adams once wrote that other countries should be aware that no one serving in United States government bodies ever "had interviews with the gods, or were in any degree under the influence of Heaven, more than those at work upon ships or houses, or laboring in merchandise or agriculture; it will forever be acknowledged that these governments were contrived merely by the use of reason and the senses."[93]

Among all their achievements, Jefferson and Adams were known to be personally proudest of their role "in establishing a secular government whose legislators would never be required, or permitted, to rule on the legality of theological views," historian Susan Jacoby wrote in *Freethinkers: A History of American Secularism* (2004).[94]

In an 1819 letter, Madison dismissed the "universal opinion" of preceding centuries that religion and clergy would collapse without government support. He said Virginia's success under its smoothly functioning secular government "conspicuously corroborates the disproof" of that fear. In the meantime, he pointed out, "the number, the industry, and the morality of the Priesthood, & the devotion of the people have been manifestly increased by the total separation of the Church from the State."[95]

Then newly elected, President Jefferson himself coined his "wall of separation" phrase in a famous 1801 letter to the Danbury (Connecticut) Baptist Association. He was responding to Baptists' fears that religious freedom was not specified in their state's constitution. Jefferson wrote, "I contemplate with sovereign reverence that act of the whole American people which declared that their legislature should 'make no law respecting an establishment of religion, or prohibiting the free exercise thereof,' thus building a wall of separation between church and State."

'SHUT THE EYE OF REASON'

The founders were eminently reasonable, practical, non-superstitious men, although some were undoubtedly and incongruently devout Christians. Colonial American icon and fellow Founding Father Benjamin Franklin likely spoke for most if not all of them when he wrote in his popular *Poor Richard's Almanac*: "The way to see by faith is to shut the eye of reason."

Even elsewhere, political thinkers understood what made the American secular experiment in government special. But there's also been a fair amount of misquoting over the years. For example, there's this quote below, falsely attributed to renowned English philosopher and political economist John Stuart Mill (1806–1873) by American blogger and podcaster "John Mill," the radio persona of Ronald Bruce Meyer. But it's still relevant in modern America as white Christian nationalism periodically becomes ascendant in national politics, and it's also true:

> *The United States is no more a Christian nation because most of its citizens are Christians than it is a 'white' nation because most of its citizens are white. We are Americans because we practice democracy and believe in republican government, not because we practice revealed religion and believe in Bible-based government.*[96]

Acutely aware of the existential dangers of religious tyranny and believing spiritual freedom was the only rational solution, the founders demanded wholly secular rather than Christian governance for their new republic.

"*By the all-powerful dispensations of Providence, I have been protected beyond all human probability and expectation; for I had four bullets through my coat, and two horses shot under me, yet escaped unhurt, altho' death was levelling my companions on every side.*"

— **George Washington** (1732–1799),
then would-be commander-in-chief of American
forces in the Revolutionary War and eventual first US
President, in a letter to his brother John in 1755

CHAPTER 10

REVOLUTION

After independence, a resurgence of faith

LTHOUGH THE FOUNDERS were enthusiastic about creating a secular American government, that is not to say that religion did not play a role in the eventual Revolutionary War (1775–1783). It did—a markedly influential one.

Contentious religious loyalties marked the American Revolution against Great Britain, as they had in the eighteenth-century French Revolution, when insurrectionists attacked the Catholic clergy as energetically as they did the king.

Most colonial clergy supported American independence, and more than one hundred of them reportedly served as chaplains in the Continental Army. But a smaller number of colonial Anglican ministers affiliated with the Church of England were loyalists to the crown and some even subsequently embedded with British troops. One Anglican loyalist preacher, Jonathan Boucher, warned colonists of the need to "obey constituted authority" while fully realizing these were fighting words among American revolutionaries.

"Concerned about his safety in proclaiming such an unpopular view, [Boucher] carried into his pulpit not only his sermon manuscript but also a loaded pistol," after hostilities with England heated up on the eve of the Revolutionary War, according to an article in the online *Christian Times*.[97]

WAR CLOUDS

Despite the colonies' impetus toward secular government, religion was still a significant factor as war clouds gathered. The Continental Congress called for a day of prayer and fasting, and ministers used the occasion to whip up colonists' support for independence. The Congress ordered that copies of the Declaration of Independence be delivered first not to government or newspaper offices but to clergy—and they were required to read it to their congregations the first Sunday after they received it.

Even war needs marketing support.

As with all American wars from the Revolution onward (perhaps with most wars everywhere), leaders frame the conflict as a battle of good (us) versus evil (them). In the War of Independence, the "good guys" were colonial Christians of eminently American Protestant sects. The enemy was comprised of invading English soldiers and colonists who supported England's King George III and/or the Anglican Church (Church of England) he personi-fied and headed. Virtually everybody loathed Catholics (except Catholics and "High" Anglican churchgoers, who leaned more toward Catholicism than Protestantism).

So religion gave Americans moral justification against the British, and one scholar contends that the colonies' Christian clergy did a lot of the heavy lifting to prepare for the fight. They did this "by turning colonial resistance into a righteous cause, and by crying the message to all ranks in all parts of the colonies, ministers did the work of secular radicalism and did it better."[98] Presbyterian minister James Caldwell reportedly helped out at the 1780 battle of Springfield, New Jersey, by grabbing some paper hymnals at a nearby church to provide ammunition wadding for patriot muskets.[99]

In fact, being Anglican became tantamount to being a traitor. When the Continental Congress in 1775–76 issued decrees ordering American churches to fast and pray for colonial patriots, it also decreed, along with several states, that praying for the British king and Parliament were treasonous.[100]

But many loyalist, royalist, Anglophile colonists, as members of the Church of England, nonetheless chafed against the radicalism of anti-British colonial patriots who worshipped with independent, non-Anglican Protes-tant sects. Even pastors of various sects fought enthusiastically in the war, some even commanding soldiers. Pacifist Quakers, on the other hand, added to the chaos by refusing on religious grounds to fight on either side. Religious inscriptions adorned many colonial battle flags during the Revolutionary War. As in the future Civil War, families in the Revolution, not to mention entire communities, were routinely split over the flammable mix of religion, blood ties, and politics.

After the Revolution, American Anglican parishes loyal to the king of England (the church sovereign) "shattered" when their financial support disappeared. Many of the church's pastors fled, mainly back to England with thousands of congregants, and many church buildings were damaged or destroyed before and during the war, wrote Powell Mills Dawley in "Our Christian Heritage."[101] In fact, Anglican churches in America had long sought more independence from faraway bishops in England, vexed by imperious prelates the Church of England sent to the colonies to oversee their churches. The Revolution simply quickened their ultimate liberation from their English ecclesiastic overlords.

Further raising colonists' ire against the British before the Revolution as colonial leaders tried to improve the virtue of citizens with religion, Americans were repulsed by the profane, bawdy and otherwise immoral behavior of British troops—largely Anglicans—who previously had been sent to America to fight in the French and Indian War.

Many other church groups besides Anglicans struggled for survival up to, during, and immediately after the Revolution during a general slide in piety, including Baptists in Virginia, Quakers and Lutherans in Pennsylvania, and various Presbyterian-Congregationalists and Dutch and German reform denominations. None were aware that a spike in Christian piety would soon follow the war's end.

POST-WAR RELIGIOUS REASSESSMENT

As the Revolution concluded and both state and federal governments began to embrace the religious freedom motif and to end church-state entanglements, a number of states—New York, Maryland, North and South Carolina, and Virginia—severed their colonial Church of England legal tethers. Funding thus dried up for Anglican congregations.

Surviving Anglican-style congregations in the colonies after the Revolution reinvented themselves as "Episcopal," meaning bishop-led and aligned with the Church of Scotland (a separatist, offshoot of the Church of England and not beholden to the king), as opposed to "Presbyterian," non-Anglican Protestant church groups led by local ministers and elders. American Episcopal congregations had existed in the colonies since Jamestown, along with formal Anglican churches.

As the concept of church-state separation evolved in the post-war colonies and public funds for churches largely vanished, the new hybrid Episcopal Church adopted revisions in the Anglican Book of Common Prayer more compatible with evolving American democratic ideals.[102] This, of course, required removing the traditional prayer to the king. The American Episcopalians also unsuccessfully sought authorization from the English church to operate independently.

In 1789, formerly Church of England-aligned Episcopalian ministers in America voted to merge with the Protestant Episcopal Church of the United States.

Likewise, American Methodists, who like Episcopalians considered themselves "in communion" with colonial Anglicans, had reorganized in 1784 as the Methodist Episcopal Church.

Methodism—the term was originally pejorative, as in "method acting" in Hollywood—was a Protestant revival movement led by English theologian and evangelist John Wesley within the Church of England. In opposition to the idea of pre-ordained, divinely "elected" saints in Calvinism, Wesley preached that immortal salvation was available to all, for which Jesus Christ died on the cross, and that Christian faith positively transformed the character of the faithful. Wesley eventually opposed Methodism's control by bishops (episcopal) rather than lay panels (presbytery), although a number of Methodist sects embraced the episcopal system in America. In fact, the Methodist Episcopal Church (MEC) was the oldest and largest Methodist denomination in the United States from its founding in 1784 until 1939, and the first to organize nationally.[103]

Along with other Protestant denominations, Methodism thrived on the heels of the First and Second Great Awakenings in the early 1700s. In the twentieth century, most Methodist factions formally merged.

In colonial times, Presbyterians also reorganized their church to be more distinctly American and less influenced by the Church of Scotland. Internal American religious, ethnic, political, and cultural conflicts roiled well into the nineteenth century as the new country struggled to coalesce around shared democratic and religious principles, and an ethos of national stability.

Today, both Anglican and Episcopal church bodies coexist in the United States.

POSTWAR CHRISTIANITY

Remember, the US Constitution was not ratified by the first nine of thirteen colonies until 1788, with the rest signing on after the Bill of Rights was drafted and approved the following year (and formally ratified in 1791). The Bill of Rights provided crucial personal liberties, including barring Congress from interfering in any way with private or public religion.

So, immediately after the Revolutionary War, the constitutional ethos of religious freedom and church-state separation familiar in the US today had not yet been firmly established in the new nation.

Yet, while the Revolution didn't kill established religions in the colonies, it changed them. In some post-Revolution colonies, official state churches were still entrenched, some of these remaining vigorous even well into the nineteenth century. This lag occurred because national institutions of justice that could interpret and enforce the new Constitution's religious principles were slow to develop, and colonies long after continued to follow religious practices, like teaching Christianity in schools, which was ultimately ruled unconstitutional by modern courts despite continuing conflict among Americans regarding church-state separation.

The historically contentious, uniquely American wrestling match with diverse religious influences in schools is highlighted in the introduction's opening paragraph in University of Notre Dame historian John T. McGreevy's 2003 book, *Catholicism and American Freedom: A History*. Titled "The Elliot School Rebellion, Boston, 1859," the intro reprises a conflict between Protestant and Catholic students in reciting the Ten Commandments as required daily in all Massachusetts schools at the time along with other Bible readings. The proximate problem was that each faith's wording of the commandments differed, but the Protestant-favored King James Bible was used as the school's authoritative text for the recitations (although Catholic students inserted their own faith's words quietly in the din of voices).

The notorious Elliot School incident occurred on Monday morning, March 7, 1859, when teacher Sophia Shepard called on a Catholic youth, ten-year-old Thomas J. Whall, to recite the day's commandments. He refused because of his faith.

According to McGreevy, when the boy again refused a week later, Assistant Principal McLaurin F. Cook was called in to resolve the impasse. Castigating Whall for his refusal, McLauren reportedly said, "I will whip him till he yields if that takes the whole forenoon." After thirty minutes of whipping the boy's hand with a rattan cane, it was "cut and bleeding." But still he refused to recite. Then the principal ordered all boys to leave school who refused to recite the King James version of the commandments. One hundred boys departed that first day and three hundred the next when they brought copies of the Catholic Vulgate Commandments to read from.[104]

The short-term result of the fiasco was that a lawsuit against Cook for assault and battery, filed by Whall's father, was dismissed by the courts, which held that religious instruction was an appropriate school function, and cited the national interest the case spawned. The long-term result was that the dust-up spawned a host of Catholic parochial schools in Boston and across the country.[105]

McGreevy notes that Protestant immigrants to the North American colonies had harbored powerful anti-Catholic prejudices from the beginning, stemming from their experience with authoritarian Catholicism in Europe. For instance, he points out that Mayflower passenger William Brewster carried with him among his effects on his voyage to the New World a new English translation of Venetian historian Paulo Sarpi's "slashing attack on the Council of Trent and the papacy."

As America's religious growing pains born of diversity played out in the nation's unfurling history, from Plymouth Rock to Gettysburg to the lovely hills of California, the cultural intensity of spirituality in the country ebbed and flowed. But a series of religious phenomena starting in the 1700s proved the most consequential for the evolving American religious enterprise.

The spirit of religious reform electrified during a series of spiritual revivals in the eighteenth and nineteenth centuries disrupted business as usual among mainstream American church bodies, sparking movements for further reform and creation of new Christian sects throughout the country. New denominations pushed to reduce or eliminate public taxation for established churches not attended by all taxpayers, and to accommodate greater freedom of worship for all without government imposition—state or federal.

By the 1840s, the Methodist Episcopal Church was the largest denomination in the country, reportedly with more than a million members, and the Baptists were close behind. Methodism carried the "episcopal" tag because its founder, John Wesley, was a reformist Anglican priest, and he allied with the Church of England-related Episcopalians.

What gave Wesley's denomination its broad appeal is obvious: Wesley preached that not only could authentic faith in Jesus make every Christian believer eligible for salvation, it could *ensure* it. This happily differed with other "covenant of grace" sects, such as Calvinism, which held that only a divinely selected elite was eligible for immortality in paradise (but only God knew whom he would choose to grace the preferred list, and he unhelpfully declined to reveal it before death). Conversely, the "Methodism" method involved good works—personally extended charity and mercy for the poor, the sick and the forgotten—and the theology focused far more on saving working class people than the elite. The sect also encouraged greater emotional expression at worship services and did not mandate educational requirements for preachers.

Wesley's denomination existed in the US until 1939, when it merged with the Methodist Episcopal Church South and the Methodist Protestant Church to create the Methodist Church. Then, in 1968, it merged with the Evangelical United Brethren Church and became the still-current United Methodist Church.

CHURCH GROWTH

The end of the Revolution began a slow but inexorable growth in American church membership that would peak in the twentieth century. As the Revolutionary era ended, fewer than 20 percent of white adults reportedly constituted regular churchgoers and a far lower percentage of blacks. But over the next two centuries, membership in Christian congregations rose sharply. By 1840, between 30 percent and 40 percent of white Christians regularly attended services, increasing to more than 50 percent by the early twentieth century. The proportion surged to 65 percent in the 1950s, where it remained into the new millennia.[106]

LEGAL QUESTIONS

But first, there was the continuing problem of resolving questionable religious practices endorsed by individual states. That remains a work in progress in US courts today, including the Supreme Court.

The highest court has tended to support diverse religious freedom while not absolutely prohibiting states or communities from favoring Christianity in sometimes subtle but, arguably, insidious ways, such as official prayers (almost always Christian) opening city council meetings. In a sense, it is a continuation of a debate in the years 1784 and 1785 among Virginia lawmakers that culminated in prohibition of any official state religion and of government aid to churches. But by 1834, all state church designations in America had been eliminated.

"God forbid that I should travel with anybody a quarter of an hour without speaking of Christ to them."

— **George Whitefield** (1714–1770),
English Anglican cleric and a founder of Methodism
and the Evangelical movement who preached at
a series of revivals in America in 1740 that came
to be known as the First Great Awakening

CHAPTER II

THE GREAT AWAKENING

Wave of revivals reinvigorates the faithful

HRISTIAN PIETY AND enthusiasm certainly ebbed and flowed throughout Western history. But one of the faith's saving graces, as it were, has been that whenever it resurrected from apparent oblivion—as it often did in America—the fervor of the faithful seemed to pulse stronger than ever.

This was especially true during several periods of US religious revival known collectively as the Great Awakening.

This phenomenon of heightened Christian piety swept through the country during the early eighteenth and late nineteenth centuries as part of a similar ferment in Western Europe. At various times, such revivals offered Americans a welcome respite from anxieties and fears stemming from wars (e.g., the Revolutionary War, Civil War), economic upheavals (e.g., the Panic of 1857), and the mounting uncertainties of a fast-changing world (e.g., science was challenging religious ideas). The revivals dramatically spiked general religious interest and gusto in the United States and created new, uniquely American spiritual paradigms.

A 'DEFINING' AMERICAN MOVEMENT

It has been called "the largest, strongest, most sustained religious movement in US history," and came closest to "defining what it meant to be an insider in US culture," according to the authors of *Religion in American Life*.[107]

Unhelpfully for reason, though, the overwhelming emotionalism and anti-rationalism inherent in the Awakenings also undercut a growing awareness of the importance of evidence-based scientific pragmatism bequeathed by the Enlightenment. Many Americans in these revivals ignored material reason, ignored that sensory perception offers no undeniable confirmation that supernatural beings and realms exist, to gladly immerse themselves in self-indulgent, overweening religiosity. In some respects, the country has never fully recovered.

Mainly led by Evangelical Protestant preachers of Calvinist inclination, the revivals seemed to bathe attendees with a profound emotional sense of imminent spiritual redemption. This ecstatic heart of the "awakening" experience led to increased membership in evangelical churches and the creation of new religious crusades and denominations. Among the influential long-term consequences of the Awakenings on American society is the dramatically expansive modern *Evangelical* movement (the term, derived from Greek and Latin, roughly means "messenger of good news," as in the gospel).

Each separate awakening had its own unique flavor but the "good news" was generally spread through what were called "revival" or "camp" meetings, which sometimes drew fervent crowds numbering in the thousands. The often raucous, delirium-inducing revivalist gatherings, especially in the nineteenth century, were commonly held at remote sites offering basic, temporary accommodations that exuded the unfussy ambience of campsites. They were like small Woodstock-style concerts, with preachers serving as the over-the-top rock stars. But some early revival gatherings were also held in eastern urban venues.

The preaching ethos of the First Awakening was loud and flamboyant, but the faithful themselves were relatively passive, if spirit-filled, receptors, though not unresponsive. Believers in that awakening were encouraged to embrace their sinful guilt, strive to live pious lives and make themselves ready to accept God's grace, should he ever deign to offer it.

In the Second Great Awakening, though, preachers, often in more subdued tones, startled the faithful by insisting instead that such divine grace was already available to everyone; they only needed to open their hearts to absorb it. This idea that human beings could ensure their own salvation proved overwhelmingly seductive to many adherents. Camp meeting attendees described the feeling of the Holy Spirit entering their bodies in visceral terms. It was "like a wave of electricity," as one of the most influential preachers in the second awakening, Charles G. Finney, recalled such a conversion experience in his memoirs.[108]

Whereas existing church members were targeted by revival leaders in the First Awakening, the unchurched—especially in the remote hinterland—were specifically sought out in its second iteration.

Leading up to the Civil War and the final eruption of Christian piety in the awakening series, a fertile new religious group began to emerge—the Baptists. The evangelical sect only baptized adults (children were deemed too immature to fathom the meaning). In 1845, the sect formed the Southern Baptist Convention, purportedly to shelter slaveholders' status in the church.

All of the previous awakenings seemed to collectively gather force for the final revival beginning in the 1850s, which ultimately proved more emotionally motivating and influential in American culture than all the rest.

This is how the awakenings unfolded:

The **First Great Awakening** played out from the 1730s through about 1743, mainly targeting the urban elite and characterized by the revival preaching of British evangelist George Whitefield, who traveled to America in 1738 and again in 1739. Whitefield's revival campaign was reported by writers of the time as "triumphant from Philadelphia to New York, and back to the South,"[109] and that wherever he preached "the consequences were large and tumultuous."[110] The interlude replaced traditional, somber sermonizing with bravura orations that roused the emotions, and it marked the beginning of general acceptance of blacks—free and slave—into mainstream Christianity (beyond private, ad hoc services slave owners irregularly allowed).

The **Second Great Awakening**, in the late eighteenth through early nineteenth centuries (1795–1835), was more national but mostly centered in the Northeastern states and near frontiers to the west, such as Indiana Territory. Distinctively, this revival, which focused on less-prosperous and less-educated

Americans, was more emotionally muted than the first among evangelical preachers, but more fervently animated among its frenzied throngs of faithful. It also ushered in that "unique frontier institution known as the camp meeting'"[111] as revivalists enthralled the faithful in scattered settlements in what was then the American outback. The Second Awakening sparked a tremendous increase in church attendance and focused on soul saving. It also stimulated new social impulses, such as alcohol temperance, female emancipation, and global evangelism.[112]

The **Third Awakening**, from the 1850s into the early 1900s, had an even greater effect than the previous two on future Christianity in the US. It successfully synthesized cumulative achievements of the prior Awakenings, stimulating Christian faith in general. But it also kick-started legions of new organizations and institutions that carried the work of Christianity forward to help ensure the faith's broader interweave in the fabric of society and its robust survival in American attitudes. Among the new organizations introduced to American cities and towns during this period was the YMCA (Young Men's Christian Association), and among the new attitudes promoted was a "self-sacrificing zeal in good works."[113]

The catastrophic Civil War provided strong impetus during the revival for renewed piety and national reforms, including the founding of Christian and Sanitary commissions, and church-organized Freedmen Societies to educate newly freed slaves and their families in the South.

THE CANE RIDGE REVIVAL

Of all the countless Great Awakening events in America in two centuries, one stood head and shoulders above the rest: Cane Ridge. The momentous gathering in early August 1801 on a rural Kentucky hillside could fairly be characterized as "the mother of all Great Awakening events."

Some twenty thousand people reportedly encamped at a place called Cane Ridge (the word "cane" was evoked by bamboo stands flourishing on the hill). Many revivalists journeyed by horse-drawn wagons for many days over long distances to attend. It was "the most important religious gathering in all of American history, for what it symbolized and for the effects that flowed from it," Vanderbilt University historian emeritus Paul Keith Conklin (b. 1929) wrote in *Cane Ridge: America's Pentecost.*

The frontier Christian revival was held near Cane Ridge Meeting House in a rural area about twenty miles from Lexington, Kentucky. It proved a watershed event for American Christianity as reputedly the "largest and most famous camp meeting of the Second Awakening."[114] Hosted by Cane Ridge Presbyterian Church and its pastor, Barton W. Stone, the event was based on the Scottish tradition of "Holy Fairs" that culminated with a celebration of Christ's last supper.

The faithful gathered over about a week to attend evangelical revivalist sermons delivered by a variety of itinerant preachers. To put the crush of people in perspective, only about two thousand settlers lived in all of Kentucky at the time. Presbyterians organized the event, but it had an ecumenical flavor as numerous Methodist and Baptist preachers and others also held forth. Not surprisingly, this was a passionate event, with attendees (and preachers) weeping or falling over in religiously induced deliriums and expressing their religious feelings by *glossalia*, or "speaking in tongues," and other charismatic and ecstatic practices that would later characterize the twentieth century's fervent Pentecostal movement.

The gathering is believed by some historians to be the first true frontier camp meeting in the United States, and it stimulated a rash of other such future assemblies as well as Christian revivals of all kinds over many years.[115] Part of the reason for the extreme interest was a lack of churches and ministers at the time and, for that matter, any form of entertainment in sparsely populated rural and frontier territories.

Members of various churches in the area and their ministers were invited to participate, but interest unexpectedly snowballed and attendees quickly exceeded the capacity of the Meeting House.

Not everyone was filled with the Holy Spirit, however.

Some in attendance "stood at the edges and mocked" the proceedings, wrote Mark Galli in "Revival in Cane Ridge," an article in the Christian History Institute magazine. But most "were marveling at the wondrous hand of God."[116] Galli believes the Cane Ridge phenomenon lifted an apathy toward Christianity evident since the Revolution, particularly on the frontier, and it "ignited the explosion of Evangelical religion, which soon reached into nearly every corner of American life."

Before Cane Ridge, what few preachers existed in remote areas lamented how few practicing Christians could be found, much less lured to church. Membership in the Methodist Church, the most popular denomination among middle and lower classes, had been sharply declining nationally and in Kentucky. Adding to the problem of low membership was that leaders in diminishing congregations began banishing backsliding members for vice and other moral transgressions to purify the ranks, further eroding membership.

In fact, Americans' interest in Christianity had been generally flagging for decades up to the Cane Ridge phenomenon.

"Five years earlier, few would have predicted the Cane Ridge revival. Since the American Revolution, Christianity had been on the decline, especially on the frontier," according to a Christian History Institute article online: "Sporadic, scattered revivals—in Virginia in 1787–88, for example—dotted the landscape, but they were short-lived. Religious indifference seemed to be spreading."[117]

After traversing Kentucky not long before Cane Ridge, preacher James Smith wrote of his hope that increasing revivalist yearnings at the time would give Christianity a much-needed boost. Smith wishfully anticipated it would make the glory of scripture "shine forth hereafter with redoubled luster."[118]

The success at Cane Ridge motivated organizers to plan another gathering the following month at Gaspar Creek Church. The smaller subsequent event was equally energized, if not more, and preachers had to attend throughout the night to penitents overwhelmed by religious emotion. The need for food or sleep reportedly vanished in the revelers' abject piety.

In succeeding months revivalism spread like a virus through Kentucky and in Tennessee as well, fueled by stories in major national newspapers that enthusiastically reported the Cane Ridge event and other similar religious gatherings. After one such event at a place named Desha's Creek, attendee John McGee reported that "people fell before the Word, like corn before a storm of wind, and many rose from the dust with divine glory shining in their countenances."[119] The combined ambient noise at these gatherings included hymn singing, crying, preaching, shrieks of guilt and grief, the feral bellowing of religious abandon. The sound became so intense some described it to be like "the roar of Niagara."

However, the impassioned milieu disturbed rather than electrified many mainstream preachers. They were concerned that sermon-givers' rage against the devil and man's sinful nature was in fact just exploiting people's emotions and creating more spiritual anxiety. But it was a runaway train. With Cane Ridge, old-time religion came roaring back.

UNREASON ECLIPSES REASON

However, in terms of the serial eclipse of reason by unreason throughout Western history, the most momentous consequences of the Great Awakenings were the enormous expansion of membership in Christian churches throughout America and a broadening of religious vitality. This included the deep insinuation of mystical emotionality at the expense of Enlightenment rationality in the American mind; a proliferation of religious institutions and organizations, whose combined effects are incalculable; and the dispersal of countless random religiously affiliated bodies far and wide over the American landscape.

If there was any danger that American Christianity would slowly fade away, as it sometimes appeared it might in earlier times, the apparent risk evaporated in the serial Great Awakenings. In fact, Christianity became ever more deeply embedded in the national unconscious.

Yet, after the acute fervor of the Awakenings finally subsided, overt Protestant revivalism did ebb somewhat in the first half of the twentieth century, but tent revivals and other forms of Protestant renewal continued to be important in the South and Midwest. After World War II, though, mass evangelism was buoyed once again as revival "crusades" became popular under American evangelist Billy Graham and others.[120]

Today revivalism is much less apparent than it once was in America. But it also doesn't seem to matter in some ways. Christianity, long the nation's virtually unchallenged faith of choice, by now appears to have become so tightly interwoven in the fabric of American life that it requires little rejuvenating assistance for robust survival.

Of the roughly two billion Christians in the world today, about 285 million are Evangelicals (13 percent), or "Bible-believing Christians."[121] The majority of Evangelicals reportedly live in the Americas—the United States has the largest concentration[122]—plus Africa and Asia. Evangelicals represent 25.4 percent of all American Christians, compared to about 21 percent who are Catholic.

In America, we can at least partly credit the charismatic Awakenings with the continuing and vast perpetuation of Christian faith still very evident throughout the land. These fervent revivals not only served as an initial vaccination against objective reason but, in effect, provided periodic emotional boosters as well.

"The solemn charge which the Parliament preaches to all true believers is a return to the primitive unity of the world.... The results may be far off, but they are certain."

— **John Henry Barrow** (1847–1902),
American Presbyterian clergyman and chairman
of the General Committee on the first Congress
of Religions (later known as the World's
Parliament of Religions) in Chicago in 1893

CHAPTER 12

WORLD'S PARLIAMENT OF RELIGIONS

Diverse global faiths seek religious dialogue

THE "RESULTS" TO which John Henry Barrows refers in the adjacent quote is his vision of the eventual dominance of Christianity among world religions. But, although not a unique opinion in America at the time, it was Barrows' private bias (if also widely held among American Protestants[123]), not the aim or consensus of the first Congress of Religions, held in 1893 in the US.

Later renamed the World's Parliament of Religions, the movement's initial gathering in Chicago was the brainchild of Charles Carroll Bonney, the Swedish lay chairman of the organizing Congress Auxiliary. The Congress' initiators purportedly sought global religious understanding, but whereas international religious leaders congregated, they were not necessarily of the same mind.

Nonetheless, the parliament was viewed by members of many faiths as a gathering of monumental importance. Max Müller, a top international expert in comparative studies of religion, said the event "stands unique, stands unprecedented in the whole history of the world," and hoped it would stimulate improved religious understanding worldwide.[124]

To direct organizational efforts for the Congress, Bonney had appointed American First Presbyterian Church pastor Barrows, perhaps the most famous US preacher of his day who purportedly claimed that Abraham Lincoln only became a Christian in the middle of the Civil War. (In fact, a lifelong friend of Lincoln said he had no idea whether the spiritually opaque president was ever a Christian or not).

The Parliament was held in Chicago on the shores of Lake Michigan, part of the Columbian Exposition marking the quadrennial of Christopher Columbus' 1492 landing in the New World. Attending the Congress were international delegations representing Protestantism, Catholicism, Hinduism, Jainism, Judaism, Islam, Greek and Russian Orthodoxy, Confucianism, Taoism, Shintoism, Ethical Cultural, and other religious and spiritual traditions. The event's vision was to gather world religious leaders from the East and West, identify fundamental truths held in common, and promote brotherhood and tolerance among religions worldwide.

However, the lead-up to the Parliament was anything but smooth. The parent church of Barrow's own denomination, the Presbyterian Church of the United States, and the English Archbishop of Canterbury virulently opposed the idea on grounds that meeting equitably with other religions would imply that they were equally as authentic as Christianity (the "one true church," in the eyes of those who worshipped Jesus). Also opposed were the Sultan of Turkey, the European Roman Catholic hierarchy, and many prominent North American Evangelical leaders. International interfaith goodwill would be a process, not an immediate reality, it seemed.

Initial reservations were ultimately at least partially resolved, and some four thousand Congress delegates convened on September 11, 1893, in the Expo's Hall of Columbus. Barrows chaired and presided at most sessions. Although English-speaking Christian presenters predominated, forty-one representatives of other faiths also spoke.

In general, the Congress tried to avoid conspicuously elevating any religious tradition over another, focusing mainly on identifying similarities among divergent faiths and fostering understanding and tolerance for all. However, Michael J. Altman in his 2017 book *Heathen, Hindoo, Hindu* contends that the Parliament effectively "reinforced the American Protestant establishment."[125]

In fact, a single person, American Protestant historian G. Bonet Maury, was selected to formally represent Christianity in general. Other US Christian delegates addressed the gathering on religiously oblique or even political topics, such as women and spirituality. For example, Rev. Thomas Richey of New York, a doctor of divinity, spoke on "The Relations Between the Anglican Church and the Church of the First Ages." Rev. Annis F.F. Eastman of New York's topic was "The Influence of Women in Religion," Bishop B.W. Arnett of Ohio spoke on "Christianity and the Negro," and Marion Murdoch of Ohio talked about "A New Testament Woman."[126]

Grandstanding for particular sects was not part of the official proceedings, but delegates like Barrows stumped for Christianity in *ad hoc* ways.

It was a given among attendees that religion was universally a major component of culture and a way to understand different peoples.

"Would you ask me about the Buddhist morality?" Shaku Soyen, a Buddhist representative from Japan, asked rhetorically. "I reply, in Buddhism the source of moral authority is the causal law. Be kind, be just, be humane, be honest, if you desire to crown your future. Dishonesty, cruelty, inhumanity, will condemn you to a miserable fall."[127] His words basically summed up the Western "golden rule" as well as Eastern karma.

Some of the female delegates used the occasion to inject protests about the many ways religion disempowered women. The Rev. Mrs. Anna Eastman, a Christian delegate from East Bloomfield, New York, contended that none of the faiths represented at the Congress "has given to woman an equal place with man as the full half of the unit of humanity."[128]

Rabbi Joseph Silverman, a Jewish delegate from New York, characterized his faith as ecumenical at heart. "The Jew is tolerant... by virtue of his religious teaching. He believes in allowing every man, what he claims for himself, the right to work out his own salvation and make his own peace with God."[129]

Indian delegate Swami Vivikananda, a Hindu monk, promoted a universal creed. "If there is ever to be a universal religion," he said, "it must be one which will hold no location in place or time; which will be infinite, like the God it will preach."[130]

CHRISTIAN SUPREMACY?

Barrows and other Christians speaking at the Congress no doubt had to monitor and suppress their deep sense of a natural Christian supremacy in the world.

In a post-Congress article regarding the event, Barrows revealed his bias that, "'Human progress' would objectively reach its culmination through Christianity. As the apex of all religions, Christianity can influence other religions meaningfully, but not vice versa…. The Parliament has shown that Christianity is still the great quickener of humanity, that it is now educating those who do not accept its doctrines…"[131]

Altman noted in *Heathen*, "Despite their differences, all the members of this sacred cavalcade were part of a grand intermingling of religions… a gathering under the star of Christianity, whose steady beaming draws wise men of the East to the unfading brightness and growing splendor of the Prince of Peace."[132]

At the opening of the Congress' first session, a US Catholic cardinal led delegates in the Lord's Prayer—Barrow later claimed, again unilaterally, that it became the event's "universal prayer"—and thereafter the prayer opened festivities on each of the Parliament's seventeen days.

Even so, the Congress resulted in a significant leveling legacy. It encouraged American acceptance of the academic study of comparative religion—religious studies" became one of the first academic disciplines in the modern era—and raised awareness of spiritual diversity worldwide as well as religious pluralism in the US. It also contributed to the global ecumenical movement that began in the twentieth century to bring Christian denominations together to help promote faith, hope and charity as well as material support for millions of suffering human beings devastated by global wars and other catastrophes.

Contemporary Anglican priest and author Marcus Braybrooke wrote that the 1893 Congress remains "a remarkable pioneer event, and no subsequent inter-faith gathering has come near to it in size or complexity."[133] More than seven thousand attended closing ceremonies on the final day, when delegates sang the Christianity-themed "Hallelujah Chorus" from Handel's Messiah.

Although sentiments of a cosmic or universal faith wafted about the Congress, especially from adherents of Eastern religions, the Americans generally did not see the fundamental need for the other faiths. As Barrows wrote later, "the elements of such a religion are already contained in the Christian ideal and the Christian Scripture."[134] The Congress was a nice gesture by America, but Christians couldn't actually shake their sense that already "ideal" Christianity would inform all the other non-ideal religions and not the other way around.

Richard H. Seager, an expert on the 1983 Congress in Chicago, characterized the event as an Indian summer that was "quickly banished from our collective memory."[135] No matter; any sense of global cohesion vanished in World War I anyway.

However, the ecumenical spirit of the first Congress did not disappear forever. In the 1930s, Japan held an interfaith gathering—the Great Religious Exposition—for religious groups across Japan and China. The Parliament of the World's Religions didn't formally convene again until its centenary in 1993. Thereafter, the organization only gathered sporadically through 2016.

Delegates at the 1993 event, held in Chicago, drafted a collective statement titled *Towards a Global Ethic: An Initial Declaration*, which was signed by many of the seven thousand attendees. Also at that meeting, Parliament staff published a book, *Gifts of Service to the World*, spotlighting three hundred global projects that were generating significant positive effects in the world.

At the next gathering, in 1999 in Cape Town, South Africa, delegates spotlighted the AIDS crisis in South Africa and beyond. Attendees emphasized how religious and spiritual traditions help mitigate such serious global issues.

During the 2004 Parliament in Barcelona, Spain, as part of the Universal Forum of Cultures, delegates focused on lessening religiously motivated violence, increasing access to clean water, aiding international refugees, and ending developing countries' external debt. Attendees were urged to commit to working on at least one of these problems. Parliament delegates attended the follow-up Forum Monterrey (Mexico) 2007, which focused on ending poverty across the globe.

Aboriginal reconciliation and issues of sustainability and climate change were highlighted at the formal Parliament of the World's Religions in Melbourne, Australia, in 2009.

Delegates discussed promoting world peace and justice with interfaith and cross-cultural collaboration, and envisioning new responses to religious extremism and violence.

An unusually large, five-day Parliament convened in Salt Lake City, Utah, in the US in 2015, with nearly ten thousand attendees, entertainers and volunteers from seventy-three countries representing thirty major religions and 548 sub-traditions. The most recent Parliament, attended by some eight thousand people, was held in 2018 in Toronto, Canada.

PART III

CONSOLIDATION, ENTRENCHMENT

"From this day forward, the millions of our school children will daily proclaim in every city and town, every village and rural schoolhouse, the dedication of our Nation and our people to the Almighty."

—President Dwight D. Eisenhower (1890–1969), upon signing the 1956 bill inserting "under God" into the Pledge of Allegiance

CHAPTER 13

ONE NATION, UNDER GOD

*Almost subliminally, Christianity
dominates modern American life*

T HE UNITED STATES today is steeped in Christianity, yet many Americans are only vaguely aware of its soaking reality (about 70 percent of the US population is Christian). This cluelessness exists because the faith's deep and broad prevalence has become so habitual—and thus largely subconscious—in the life of the nation.

Christianity's dominance in the US involves the also barely perceptible but influential way core Christian assumptions densely interweave with most Americans' shared secular assumptions. This might be loosely defined as "Christian privilege." The term describes how members of the religious majority are virtually insensible to the effect of their private ethos on everyone else, zealot and heretic alike, and to the special cultural privileges it endows on believers.

THE LEGACY OF CONSTANTINE

Weaving the majority faith into the fabric of culture has historical precedent, having stemmed, as I previously explained, from Roman Emperor Constantine's fourth-century seminal endorsement of Christianity as the state religion. Later medieval practices in the West continued to conflate ruler and church, making each integral to the state and to each other. Thus, faith, state, and society evolved in intimate congress over centuries, creating a mindset that early colonists brought to the New World with them.

From the beginning, Americans continuously attempted to create what Benjamin Franklin called a "Publik Religion," that is a suffusion of religious language, imagery, and spirit in civic activities throughout the country.[136] This thinking symbolized for Americans a sense of the new nation's *exceptionalism*, in which Christianity was perceived as a fundamental source of the country's republican promise and power. From this sprang "Manifest Destiny," a Christianity-tinged conceit that God intended immigrant European Americans to overrun the continent at the expense of anyone—presumably non-Christian—who got in their way.[137]

Indeed, some devout citizens were so caught up in the idea of their country's monolithic specialness they even believed that the prophesied millennial "End Times"—Judgment Day—would occur in America.[138]

'IN GOD WE TRUST'

In today's United States, organized Christianity remains hard at work, overtly and covertly, attempting to shape public attitudes and appearances to align with scripture. Most Americans hardly notice the phrase "under God" anymore in various public oaths, such as the Boy Scout pledge. Public speeches are riddled with scriptural references, church bells ring on Sundays, and the YMCAs and YWCAs have existed for so long in most of our cities and towns they now seem secular.

Despite clear constitutional issues, "In God We Trust" has been featured on US paper currency since 1957. The phrase first appeared on some coins in 1864 during the Civil War and continued periodically through late in the nineteenth century. As of 1938 the motto became stamped on *all* US coins, which continues to this day.[139] It also adorns walls behind judges' benches in US courts, is inscribed on our money, is even emblazoned on government vehicles in some jurisdictions and on license plates, and, following US Supreme Court approval, it is now also being displayed in many US school buildings.

Christianity also infuses our cultural art, a good example being the uber-American "Battle Hymn of the Republic," written by Julia Ward Howe and published in the first years of the Civil War. The lyrics, set to the melody of "John Brown's Body," are a scripture-infused memorial to the namesake's failed guerilla insurgency against Southern slavery leading up to the Civil War. The lyrics heavily entwine God and country, and the opening stanza glorifies the brutal attacks Brown's paramilitary forces made on Southerners: "Mine eyes have seen the glory of the coming of the Lord; He is trampling out the vintage where the grapes of wrath are stored."

WHY IT'S STILL WITH US

The nation's impulse to co-opt Christianity for patriotic purposes long continued into the modern era. In 1956, with America in the throes of the Cold War and still reeling from the anti-Communism terrors of McCarthyism, the government wanted to clearly distinguish the country from Soviet state atheism. Consequently, the 84th Congress declared and President Eisenhower concurred that "In God We Trust" would be the new official national motto. In 2006 (the motto's fiftieth anniversary) the US Senate reaffirmed its official status, and the US House followed suit in 2011. The 396–9 vote was arguably unconstitutional, especially considering Thomas Jefferson's insistence that American believers in "no God" have the same right as anyone else to not have religion imposed on them (e.g., on their money).

Yet today, other religious stowaways remain in civic rituals from our hyper-Christian colonial past. Take the presidential inauguration. When George Washington, an ardent church-state separatist, was sworn in as the new secular republic's first president, he incongruously put his hand on the Bible and dutifully uttered the phrase, "So help me God." Thus began an official government tradition—nowhere to be seen in the Constitution, US law, or presidential requirements—that has been followed by many if not most subsequent presidents.

Those who are believed to have *not* placed hands on bibles during swearing-in ceremonies include Teddy Roosevelt, who was very quickly sworn after William McKinley was assassinated, according to official records kept by the architect of the Capitol, and John Quincy Adams who, according to his letters, instead used a law book to symbolize his secular nature. Lyndon Johnson is rumored to have used Jacqueline Kennedy's Catholic missal aboard Air Force One. There's no concrete evidence that Rutherford Hayes or Calvin Coolidge used a book of any kind for their oaths, as indeed there isn't for any early president from John Adams through John Tyler.[140]

Barack Obama placed his hand on two bibles when he was sworn in to his second term in 2013: the one used by sixteenth president Abraham Lincoln in 1861, (the first time it had been used for the purpose since Lincoln's inauguration), and assassinated civil-rights leader Martin Luther King, Jr.'s "traveling Bible."[141]

THE MONKEY TRIAL

The divide between fundamentalist, literalist Christianity and more populous mainstream or "modernist" pro-science redoubts of American Christian culture opened wide in 1925 with the famous Scopes "Monkey Trial" in Tennessee. In the trial, biology teacher John Scopes was convicted of violating a state law by teaching ideas—evolution in this case—that conflicted with the Bible.

The genesis of the case was a prior campaign by state Rep. John W. Butler, a Tennessee farmer and leader of the World Christian Fundamentals Association, to encourage state legislatures to establish anti-evolution laws. Tennessee ultimately complied by passing the Butler Act. Later Butler admitted that he "Didn't know anything about evolution…. I'd read in the papers that boys and girls were coming home from school and telling their fathers and mothers that the Bible was all nonsense."[142] Alarmed by Tennessee's anti-evolution law and state establishment of religious teaching, the American

Civil Liberties Union consequently financed the test case in which Scopes agreed to be prosecuted for violating the Butler Act.

During the trial, many across the country ridiculed the Tennessee position. Even so, the judge ultimately ruled that Scopes had broken the existing law, but he fined him only a nominal one hundred dollars. Many years later, in 1967, Tennessee's anti-evolution law was finally repealed.

After the trial, fundamentalists, reeling from nationwide negative attention to their cause, retreated into their own silos and continued their efforts via grassroots politics to deeply enmesh Christianity with American culture. Fundamentalists birthed the politically aggressive Christian Right in the 1980s that attempted to disingenuously insert biblical concepts (e.g., "creationism" and "creation science") into public-school science curricula.

Some prominent clergy envisioned that the twentieth century would be a boom time for Protestantism in America. Those years did see some Protestant sects gaining ground including fundamentalist Evangelicals, tongue-talking Pentecostalists (one of the fastest-growing sects in the world today), American-bred Mormonism adherents, and others. However, the century turned out to be better for Catholics, whose numbers increased exponentially during that period.

In 1900, America's ten million Catholics comprised less than 14 percent of the population, but by 2017 about a quarter of the population was Catholic, a proportion that had held roughly constant for decades.[143] Although today the faith is losing more members to other religions than they gained from such religious shifting in the past (possibly due to priestly pedophilia scandals), Catholicism is greatly benefitting from immigration, especially from Latin America, whose citizens are predominantly Catholic.[144]

The twentieth century also brought a dramatic expansion of the spirit of ecumenical (i.e. interdenominational) cooperation among churches in the United States. The so-named "ecumenical movement" was not cohesive or interfaith, but predominantly Christian, with several independent strands separately involving Catholics, Protestants, and the Eastern Orthodox Church.

In one strand, the Catholic Church, promoting theological arguments, tried to retrieve Christians who had abandoned the ancient faith for other denominations. Another strand was symbolized by the 1910 World

Missionary Conference in Edinburgh, Scotland, to which Protestant denominations and missionary groups in North America and Northern Europe sent some 1,200 delegates (no Catholic or Orthodox representatives were invited). The stated theme of Protestant gatherings was "The Evangelization of the World in This Generation." A third strand involved a 1920 Eastern Orthodox ecumenical encyclical titled "To the Churches of Christ Everywhere." The initiative sought to bring all Christian churches together under an organization akin to the United Nations.

A SLIDE IN RELIGIOSITY

Despite the steadily growing Christian population in America throughout most of the twentieth century, signs have emerged in the past few decades that those gains are fading fast overall.

From 2007 to 2014 alone, the percentage of self-professed Christians among Americans dropped precipitously from 78.4 percent to 70.6 percent (a proportion expected to descend to 66 percent by 2050). Meanwhile, the percentage of people unaffiliated with any religion—including atheists and agnostics—rose sharply from 16.1 percent of the population in 2007 to 22.8 percent in 2016 (a 6.7 percent jump). This indicates the Christian erosion may quicken in the US as increasing number of nonbelievers add their likely-to-be-unbelieving children to the population over coming generations.[145]

"It's remarkably widespread," said Alan Cooperman, director of religion research for the Pew Research Center, of the growth of the religiously unaffiliated, also known as "nones." The country is becoming less religious as a whole, and it's happening across the board."[146]

But while secularization is evident on both sides of the Atlantic, unaffiliated Americans are much more likely than their European brethren to pray and to believe in God, as US Christians are more manifestly religious than Christians throughout Western Europe. In fact, even secular American "nones" are seen to behave *as* religiously—if not more so—than Christians in a number of European countries, including France, Germany and the UK.[147]

Growth in religious disinterest is apparent across Western Europe. That region's expanding religiously unaffiliated population now ranges (compared to 22.8 percent in America) from 15 percent in uber-Catholic Italy, home of the pope, to a high of 48 percent in the long-Protestant Netherlands, followed by Norway (43 percent) and Sweden (42 percent). Some others: United Kingdom (23 percent), Germany (24 percent), and France (28 percent).[148]

While the number of Christians in the world more than tripled (by about six hundred million) to roughly two billion adherents during the last century, the global population also more than tripled (to about seven billion), leaving Christians in 2015 with the same approximate top third of the world's faithful (31.2 percent in 2015). Muslims are in second place (24.1 percent), although they boast a slightly higher birth rate than Christians. Africa and Latin America are the projected future growth centers for Christianity, not the industrialized West. Still, while Europe and the Americas continue to contain the majority of the world's Christians (63 percent) overall, it's an enormous drop from the start of the twentieth century, when that proportion was a robust 93 percent.[149]

In the past fifty years or so, American Christian missionaries have spread over the globe to preach their evangelical message, save souls, and establish religious congregations. As a result, by 2010 nearly 70 percent of global Evangelicals lived in countries outside the US and Europe, according to Duke University American Studies professor Melani McAlister in her 2018 book, *The Kingdom of God has No Borders: A Global History*.[150]

As American Evangelicals began to interact more with people in the global South, including Africa, the Caribbean, and Latin America ("Latin" because of Latinate Catholic influence in the New World during the Age of Discovery), those region's more charismatic faith styles then influenced a bump in Pentacostal-style worship—e.g., "speaking in tongues"—in America. Pentecostal denominations are currently the fastest growing in the US.

Concurrently with these shifts, US Evangelicals became better organized and acquired more political clout with such organizations at Jerry Falwell's Moral Majority and others. The evangelical vote was an important component of Donald Trump's election as US president in 2016, and continues to bolster his hold on power, despite relentless waves of scandal and legal issues.

Although the populations of Europe and the US still each contain roughly the same proportion of Christians—70-some percent—America is viewed, especially by Europeans, as puzzlingly devout. The reason for this is perhaps how differently Christians in each region view their faith. German sociologist Hans Joas in 2009 observed that "It is widely accepted that the United States is far more religious than practically any comparable European state." Research seems to bear this out. In a recent survey, 60 percent of self-described American Christians claimed their faith was "very important" in their lives, while only 21 percent of Western Europeans did.[151]

This erosion of faith in Europe has been ongoing since early in the twentieth century, when Europe was home to a majority of the world's Christians—66 percent—and North America was then a far second at 15 percent. By 2010, Europeans comprised only 25.5 percent of Christians internationally. North America, 12.3 percent. Those figures are projected to drop further by 2050: to, respectively, 15.6 percent and 9.8 percent.[152]

The number of regular churchgoers is also clearly eroding in America as the religious population ages and the young show far less interest in faith than their elders, threatening survival of many Christian sects' congregations. A 2003 Gallop poll showed that 39 percent of Americans then attended church services regularly; this compared to an average of less than 20 percent for nearly all other major Western nations, including single digits in Scandinavia, and just 1 percent in Great Britain.[153]

Material signs of erosion in faith are also far more pronounced in Europe than in America, as hundreds of churches have already closed or are existentially threatened by plummeting membership. The *Wall Street Journal* reported that about twenty Church of England congregations have been closing each year recently, Germany's Roman Catholic Church body has shuttered 515 churches in the past decade, and two hundred Danish churches of late have been ruled underused or nonviable. But the Netherlands appears to be a worst-case scenario: Two-thirds of the Netherlands' 1,600 churches reportedly will be unusable in ten years, and seven hundred Protestant churches are projected to lock up in four.[154]

The destructive attrition is deeply worrisome to the faithful in both the American and European heartlands, who fear the same dispiriting downside. "In these little towns, you have a cafe, a church and a few houses—and that is the village," says Lilian Grootswagers, an activist who fought to save the church in her Dutch town, as quoted in the *Wall Street Journal*. "If the church is abandoned, we will have a huge change in our country."

Despite general ebbing of supernatural belief in the US, a 2014 Pew survey indicated that American Christians still exhibit strong if steeply declining belief in their faith's divine elements. At that time, more than 75 percent of the faithful were still "absolutely certain" God exists (a sharp downturn from 92 percent in 2007), while 85 percent believed in heaven and 70 percent in hell.[155]

Indications are that the US is going the way of more religiously skeptical Europe—the source of our culture, after all—just a bit more slowly.

CHRISTIAN PRIVILEGE

Let's take a more comprehensive look at the phenomenon of "Christian Privilege."

Social-justice author Warren J. Blumenfeld defined the phenomenon as a system of advantages Christians enjoy in some Christian-majority societies, including, especially, the United States. The roots of this are in the presumption that the collective wishes of the dominant faith comprise an accepted social norm for *everyone*. It is a privilege that can effectively marginalize cultural and religious practices of non-Christians—e.g., Jews, Hindus, and Muslims—if not foster overt discrimination, prejudice and persecution against them.[156]

Such Christian practices include annual public, even civic, activities with religious themes, such as the Easter Egg Hunt annually hosted by the US president and the extravagant yearly observation of Christmas in virtually every small-town square, city shopping district, and most private residences in America. Other faiths, of course, are free to celebrate their own special religious days—and do—but still they cannot fully escape the often ubiquitous, very public Christian ones.

Making the problem of Christian Privilege murkier is that members of the dominant group are generally unaware of how their religion, by lording it over the broader culture, necessarily discriminates against others. Outsiders are further disempowered by cultural no-nos. Among the most egregious examples is the American cultural taboo against criticizing *any* religion, which because Christianity is by far the most common American religion, serves primarily to make any sharp critique of that particular faith seem completely inappropriate in American culture.

This societal reticence serves to shield Christianity from critical analysis in America and further reinforce and perpetuate its unverifiable beliefs.

In the same way, notes Seton Hall University psychology professor and author Lewis Z. Schlosser, protesting Christian privilege itself thus also violates a "sacred taboo." He wrote that majority pushback against attacks on this privilege is "quite similar to the way in which whites and men continue to ensure the privilege of their racial and gender groups."[157]

SUPREME BIAS

United States Supreme Court justices sometimes have been dismayingly supportive of religion's intrusion into American public life, beyond just trying to accommodate bland ecumenical prayers at civic events, like city council meetings.

Indeed, the late Supreme Court Justice Antonin Scalia, a self-described "devout Catholic," once proclaimed, "Government—however you want to limit that concept—derives its moral authority from God."[158] Clearly, Scalia's statement, regardless if it reflects historical habits of viewing God as the moral foundation of government, is still an unsubstantiated religious assumption (however widely assumed in history)—a bias, not a fact, since substantiation requires that God actually be demonstrated to exist. Thus, it is arguably not a valid material premise for a rule of law. This seems an especially fair conclusion considering that America's Founding Fathers pointedly tried to exclude the mandates of a personal God from the nation's seminal documents.

Fortunately, among top justices there is dissension concerning religion's presence in American culture and practices. In 2014, the court's majority opinion endorsed the appropriateness of formal Christian prayers at a city's public meetings (*Greece v. Galloway*). Justice Elena Kagan dissented, arguing that the subject prayers in the case, unconstitutionally, had been Christian-only for a decade. In response to one justice, who criticized her thinking as "really quite niggling," Kagan countered that that "says all there is to say" about their different views.[159]

After the ruling, *Washington Post* columnist Ruth Marcus, a Jew, also took exception to the ruling. "No member of a religious minority could possibly have written [the majority opinion]," she wrote. Although the United States is a majority Christian nation, she argued, the Constitution prohibits favoring one religion over another and "demands some sensitivity to this fact."[160] Another *Post* columnist, Richard Cohen, also a Jew, wrote, "The prayers separate." He argued the Christian prayers imply that if you're a non-Christian the venue is "not yours," that you're "an outsider—not one of them."[161]

In another case, *Elk Grove Unified School District v. Newdow*, the noncustodial father (Michael Newdow) of a girl enrolled in an Elk Grove, California, school filed suit against the district. Newdow contended the phrase "one nation, under God" that students recite daily in their Pledge of Allegiance was unconstitutional under the First Amendment's "establishment of religion" clause. A series of judgments in various courts began in 2000, and the case was finally decided by the US Supreme Court in 2005. Justice Antonin Scalia recused himself from the case because in a speech he had criticized an earlier lower-court ruling in the suit, and the remaining justices ruled 5–3 that Newdow as the noncustodial parent did not have legal standing to file the suit on behalf of his daughter. The custodial mother, a Christian who claimed her daughter was also a Christian, did not object to the pledge language.

In the suit's first decision, in 2002, the US Court of Appeals for the Ninth Circuit had ruled that the words "under God" was an endorsement of religion and thus a violation of the Constitution's establishment clause.

Although the court did not formally rule on the constitutionality of the pledge language, some justices in their written decisions spoke to the issue, indicating, dubiously, that they viewed evocation of God in this instance as historically relevant in America rather than religious. Justice William Rehnquist wrote that the term "under God" in that context is essentially secular, not endorsing religion but rather simply acknowledging the nation's religious heritage, in particular the role of religion among our Founding Fathers.

This thinking ignores the historical reality that many of the central Founders had very conflicted ideas about religion, were extremely wary of

Christian dominance in America's public life and some had complicated, agnostic—atheistic even—views of divinity itself. Yet, because the Supreme Court is supreme, its jurists clearly can rule otherwise without any acknowledgement of those contradictions. Also, it is difficult to consider the word "God" in any nonreligious context except cursing perhaps, the vagaries of history notwithstanding.

There are many other such legal cases due to the long history of Christianity in this nation, and justices on the high court sometimes tend to give religion the benefit of the doubt when it emerges contentiously in the public sphere, due to its historical commonality in the US.

RELIGIOUS INTRUSION

It's not just the Supreme Court, though. An energetic bias favoring Christianity and God at the expense of non-Christians and nonbelievers in America has enjoyed a long political and social tradition.

For example, in 2006 Louisiana Governor Bobby Jindal denigrated a US Federal Court ruling that the "under God" phrase in the Pledge of Allegiance was unconstitutional, contending that by disallowing "under God" in the Pledge the court demonstrated contempt for Congress, "which approved the language," and thus contempt for all Americans. Former Texas governor and presidential candidate Rick Perry, sees nothing wrong with prayer in schools, arguing that, after all, a chaplain leads US Senate and House members in prayer at the opening of each session (which is arguably unconstitutional in itself). Another politician, then Kansas Governor Sam Brownback, wrote in *From Power to Purpose* (2007) that when he was a US senator he viewed God—not his actual constituents—as his sole constituency. When Hurricane Katrina savaged New Orleans in 2005, Mayor Ray Nagin credited it to divine rage. "Surely God is mad at America,"[162] Nagin proclaimed.

Also after Katrina, the Rev. Franklin Graham, son of legendary American evangelist Billy Graham, was quoted by cable news channel CNN as saying, "There's been Satanic worship in New Orleans. There's been sexual perversion. God is going to use that storm to bring a revival. God has a plan. God has a purpose." Although he later denied he blamed the people of New Orleans for the catastrophe that befell their city—and prescribed more devotion to God—his explanations rang hollow.[163]

Everywhere we see that many American Christians today want to have *more* Jesus in the public sphere, not less. It is, they say, the *only* way to make the United States a more powerful, cohesive, and moral nation. Conservative Christians are now also seeking to fully legalize unfettered religious involvement in the political process by repealing the Johnson Amendment. This would allow currently illegal political endorsements from the pulpit and church funding of political candidates and organizations.

It's all part of an inexorable project of Evangelical Christianity to *terraform* America, so to speak, into a physical environment far more fertile for the faith than it is now.

PART IV

HOLDING ON

"*[Christian fundamentalists] seek to deny their children the best chance of salvation in the modern world—an understanding of it—and instead retreat into dependence on the unchanging Bible.*"

— **Matthew Chapman**,
the great-great grandson of evolution pioneer
Charles Darwin, in *40 Days and 40 Nights*

CHAPTER 14

MONKEY TRIAL REDUX

School board in 2004 votes to insert religion in science

SADLY, THE FAMOUS Scopes "Monkey Trial" in Tennessee in 1925 was not the last time Christian resistance to the time-tested science of evolution ended up in an American court.

Perpetuation of this conflict is further evidence that virtually nothing, least exhaustively verified facts, can dissuade many if not most Christian true believers—any believers in chimera, really—from jealously guarding the phantasms of their faith.

This same spiritual intransigence reemerged a little over a decade ago in the *Kitzmiller vs. Dover Area School District* case in York County, Pennsylvania. In October 2004, a majority of the Dover school board had voted that students in its schools should be "made aware of gaps/problems in Darwin's theory and of other theories of evolution including, but not limited to, intelligent design."

The board also decreed that the book *Of Pandas and People*, which specifically promotes "Intelligent Design" (i.e., biblical "creationism"), be made available to students alongside science textbooks. It was the first US school district to formally promote the teaching of so-called Intelligent Design in tandem with biological evolution in science classes.

In November the board also voted to require teachers to read the disclaimer quoted on page 126 to their ninth-grade biology classes.

A telling detail demonstrates the tenor of the atmosphere surrounding debate before the new policy's approval: the head of the curriculum committee stood up at a school board meeting and shouted, "Two thousand years ago, someone died on a cross. Can't someone take a stand for him?"[164] Ironically, this quote appears in the book *40 Days and 40 Nights* by Matthew Chapman, who attended the trial and is coincidentally the great-great-grandson of Charles Darwin (1809–1882), the originator of evolutionary theory.

Interestingly, Darwin himself was quite anxious about religion in relation to his research. And he was long fearful that publishing his scientific hypotheses on evolution would unleash debilitating criticism of his life's work by the British religious establishment and the faithful. He reportedly became a furtive, anxious agnostic while developing his theories, once mocking himself—"Oh, you Materialist!"—for believing that belief in God likely was a material (not divine) remnant of human tribal survival strategy.[165]

Barely a month after the Dover board endorsed "Intelligent Design" for the district's science classes, a group of eleven parents sued the board, arguing that teaching the concept was an unconstitutional endorsement and promotion of religion in violation of church-state separation.

The suit continued a battle that began just after the Civil War when "public"—tax-funded, government-mandated—schools were first instituted in the South. Many Southerners immediately condemned such schools as an affliction by the victorious Yankee North that they feared would empower blacks, erode the Christian religion, rob the slaver states of freedom, and breed pernicious ideas in the young. Today, the Christian Right continues to try to shield Christian children nationwide from secular ideas via private Christian schools and by promoting so-called "vouchers" that allow parents to use tax money to send their kids to such religious schools. Indeed, more than 95 percent of vouchers are used for that purpose.

This rancor also accompanied the reemergence of American Christian conservativism when President Franklin Roosevelt launched New Deal laws in the 1930s during the Depression. New Deal opponents "welded free-market economics onto Bible-based hostility to the secular democratic state," contending that the US was fundamentally a Christian nation in all aspects, including education.[166]

The *Kitzmiller vs. Dover* trial in federal district court before a notably no-nonsense jurist, Judge John E. Jones III, began September 26, 2005, and ended November 4.

In a broad, withering decision, Judge Jones, a conservative Christian Republican appointed by George W. Bush, vigorously deconstructed the plaintiffs' arguments. He dismissed Intelligent Design as reformatted "creationism," which the courts had already ruled unconstitutional. He pointedly disparaged the school board's decision as "breathtaking inanity" and said it unnecessarily caused a "legal maelstrom" that was an "utter waste of monetary and personal resources." For those reasons, Jones ruled, Intelligent Design could not legally be taught in Dover district schools. In part, he concluded:

> *The disclaimer singles out the theory of evolution for special treatment, misrepresents its status in the scientific community, causes students to doubt its validity without scientific justification, presents students with a religious alternative masquerading as a scientific theory, directs them to consult a creationist text as though it were a science resource, and instructs students to forego scientific inquiry in the public school classroom and instead to seek out religious instruction elsewhere.*[167]

Jones continued that whereas Darwin's theory of evolution and other well-tested scientific principles were not "perfect," that marginal deficit should not be used as a pretext to "to thrust an untestable alternative hypothesis grounded in religion into the science classroom or to misrepresent well-established scientific propositions."[168] He added that science experts in the trial affirmed that evolutionary theory was "overwhelmingly accepted" throughout the scientific community and that it "in no way conflicts with, nor does it deny, the existence of a divine creator."[169]

Jones seemed particularly perturbed that some Dover board proponents of the new Intelligent Design policy concealed their religious motivations in passing the science-curriculum edict. "It is ironic that several of these individuals, who so staunchly and proudly touted their religious convictions in public, would time and again lie to cover their tracks and disguise the real purpose behind the ID Policy," Jones wrote.[170]

In reference to the prior famous Scopes "Monkey Trial," the Dover case has been informally called the Dover Panda Trial.

Representing plaintiffs in the case were the American Civil Liberties Union (ACLU), Americans United for Separation of Church and State (AU) and Pepper Hamilton LLP (which receives pro bono referrals from ACLU and other public-interest groups).

The National Center for Science Education (NCSE) consulted for the plaintiffs. Defendants were represented by the Thomas More Law Center (TMLC), which bills itself as pro-life and a supporter of time-honored family values, anti-homosexuality and opposed to same-sex marriage, and a promoter of Judeo-Christian heritage and moral values.

The month after Jones' decision, Dover school district electors tossed out eight of the nine pro-Intelligent Design school board members in a regular election, installing candidates firmly opposed to that religious ideology being taught in district schools.

Still, conservative Christians elsewhere in America continue trying to insert religion in public schools. For example, legislators in South Dakota in 2017 tried—and failed—to pass legislation legally authorizing the state's schoolteachers to teach so-called "creationism," a supernatural religious concept, alongside long-established scientific evolution instruction in science classes.

That same year, Florida's Republican Governor Rick Scott signed legislation requiring his state's school districts to hire an "unbiased hearing officer" to field public complaints about educational materials used in the schools, such as books and films. These officers will have the authority to ban specific materials if they deem them somehow unsuitable or offensive, such as when Christians may be offended by science texts that contain necessarily Bible-contrary principles of evolution and global warming.

THE GOOD NEWS CLUB

In her 2017 book, *The Good News Club: The Religious Right's Stealth Assault on America's Children*, Katherine Stewart lays out an exhaustively researched exposé on how the Christian Right is covertly inserting religious proselytizing into US schools through the disingenuously titled and nationally funded "Good News Club" program.

Granted legal access to American public schools by moot recent court decisions, including by the Supreme Court, the club now operates in 3,500 school buildings, surgically targeting students aged four to fourteen (the prime indoctrination-friendly "window"), Stewart claims. The club promotes sectarian evangelical Christian theology under the guise of "nondenominational" Bible study.

Stewart charges that this program reveals a core goal of conservative evangelical Christians in the US: to weaken the secular nature of public schools—even abolish them—by embedding and spreading Christianity within their walls. She believes the campaign ultimately seeks to have Christian leaders take over schools and have Christians running them. This drive derives, she notes, from the wishful but bogus idea that America was created to be and should always remain a "Christian nation."

The schools-focused religious movement "rejects the values of inclusivity and diversity" and seeks "to undermine the foundations of modern secular democracy," Stewart wrote. "It has set its sights on destroying the system of public education—and it is succeeding."[171]

So, the stealth campaign continues.

Interestingly, the "Dover Panda Trial" lasted exactly forty days (and forty nights)—the length of Jesus' legendary self-imposed exile in the Judean Desert. The irony was pointed out in jest to Judge Jones by plaintiffs' attorney Patrick Gillen.

Jones called the conflation "an interesting coincidence." But, "It was not by design," he playfully added.

"*Many white supremacist groups adhere to the Christian Identity belief system, which holds that the world is on the verge of a final apocalyptic struggle… and teaches that the white race is the chosen race of God.*"

—**Louis Freeh**,
Former FBI director from 1993 to 2001

CHAPTER 15

CHRISTIAN IDENTITY

*Militant Christians coalesce around
race, faith, and politics*

RATHER THAN RATIONALLY reconsidering the ghostly imaginings of their faith in the secularizing present, many committed Christians have chosen instead to double down on their ancient dogmas.

Some Christian communities are becoming ever tighter, their doctrines narrower and more defensive, isolating them further not only from mainstream Christianity but also diverse Americans at large.

Too often this type of insularity results in uncomprehending and thus unapologetic irrationality of the type that gave us the Scopes and Dover, PA, trials. It also has resulted in the emergence of fringe groups that execute violent and terrorist acts within the US, such as the murder and maiming of doctors and supporters who participate in legal abortions. At least eleven abortion providers and staff members have been murdered in the US since 1993,[172] and scores of terrorist bombings and arson attacks at clinics have occurred since 1977.

This type of religious extremism also results in children being enrolled in Christian parochial schools or homeschooled, generally far away from the reason-enhancing effects of philosophy and real life, which is naturally diverse and often contentious.

But homeschooling is not a monolithic, unvarying reality, as I was informed by a friend who was homeschooled as a child yet later earned a PhD in history from Harvard. Although he described homeschooling as a "truly dangerous system," he said "it is also far more complicated and nuanced" than it may appear to the general public. He said while being homeschooled, he had enrolled in some excellent "co-op" philosophy classes taught by "incredible professors" via a local college. He added that his sister, who had the same homeschooling experience as he did, also earned a doctorate and is now a professor at a US university. My friend pointed out that he could also give "numerous counter-examples" of homeschooled kids who *hadn't* thrived in secular academic environments as he and his sister had.

But disassociation with the secular world is often the goal of fundamentalist religious enclaves.

Some fringe groups, such as the so-called Christian Identity movement, are so remote from mainstream American Christianity that they even have no meaningful collaboration or shared values with more conventional Christian groups. The FBI, which tracks terror acts related to the movement, has characterized Christian Identity adherents as only nominally Christian, espousing a fundamentalist, literalist Protestant faith and justifying their actions by referring to scripture. It continues that they are essentially followers of a racist, white-supremacist, anti-Jew, and anti-African American ideology.

This group differs significantly in their biblical interpretations from more mainstream Christians, such as in their belief that Caucasians are God's chosen race, Americans are the chosen people, and that Jews are the enemies of God.

Some Christian Identity sects mirror, though imperfectly, ideas of a nineteenth-century British movement holding that Anglo-Saxons and other whites are the descendants of biblical Israelites and that England is the true Jerusalem. Under American Christian Identity, though, the US is now viewed as the true Israel. According to movement apostles, truths hidden in the Bible are only obvious and comprehensible to white Protestants and not others.

The white race began in the Garden of Eden, according to movement interpretations of scripture, and whites were created with more ability and sophistication than any future races that might arise. Because proponents believe whites were specifically created to fight Satan on Earth for God, the race was divinely commanded to be kept separate and pure from others. And to understand the motivations of Identity proponents, it's important to note that they commonly view government as an agent of Satan in any world-ending conflagration.

The modern Christian Identity movement and many conservatives still believe that US law guarantees greater state and less federal sovereignty than is commonly assumed by American courts today ruling on constitutional issues. They also incorrectly believe America's foundational documents promote Christianity. Whenever religion is mentioned in the Constitution, for example, it is as an absolute freedom the federal government cannot impinge. Not as a Christian founding principle of the American nation.

RUBY RIDGE

Identity proponents also commonly believe that the Apocalypse—the Last Days of humankind and return of Christ espoused in the Bible—is imminent.

That was the belief of anti-government militant Randy Weaver and his Apocalyptic-Christian wife, Vicky, which lit the fuse of tragedy in 1992 on their remote mountaintop compound in Idaho known as Ruby Ridge. Killed in that lethal convergence of the Weavers, religion and federal agents were Vicky, the Weaver's fourteen-year-old son, Samuel, their dog, and family friend Kevin Harris, as well as deputy US Marshall, William Degan. The federal agents had traveled to Ruby Ridge to arrest Weaver for failing to appear in court on a charge of selling two illegal sawed-off shotguns.

The legal threads of the Weaver case are less relevant to this book than the unverifiable supernatural assumptions that caused them to lethally unfold: The idea that Judgment Day was upon us and God wanted American white people to battle the US government (the "antichrist") to cleanse the earth for Christ's return.

Thus can unsubstantiated religious notions have tragic, real-world consequences.

Christian Identity is a prime example of how such ideas can arbitrarily corrupt traditional doctrine and be used to justify manifestly un-Christian behavior: racism, intolerance, demonization, murder, and demagoguery. To glorify hatred under the guise of kindly religion.

This is not to say that religious faith, zealous or not, has only negative consequences. Certainly, Christianity, for example, has bequeathed a lot of good in the world over millennia. But the point is that believing ideas that are not verifiably true, and executing these imaginings not only as if they were true but also utterly essential to the world, can be terribly dangerous. The behavior of suicidal, self-destructive, apocalyptic cults powerfully attest to this tendency (e.g., Heaven's Gate, the Church Universal and Triumphant, People's Tempe, etc.).[173]

Although fewer than several thousand committed Christian Identity adherents are believed active nationwide, including members of such supremacist groups as the Aryan Nation, they have had an outsized impact. Proponents have been involved in a string of robberies; bombings; murders of federal officers, blacks and Jews; counterfeiting; tax rebellions and threats against IRS agents.

Supernatural belief, as history extravagantly demonstrates, all too often can lead to aggression and tragedy.

"[T]hey were all filled with the Holy Spirit and began to speak in other tongues, as the Spirit gave them utterance."

— Acts of the Apostles 2:4,
after the Holy Spirit descended on Jesus'
followers in the Pentecost, following Jesus'
purported death, resurrection and ascension

CHAPTER 16

SPEAKING IN TONGUES

*Charismatic Christianity is the
world's fastest growing sect*

O N JANUARY 1, 1901, Agnes Oznam, a thirty-one-year-old student at clergyman Charles Fox Parnham's Bethel Bible School in Topeka, Kansas, purportedly began speaking in an alien language unknown even to her, after someone (probably Parnham) placed hands on her head.

Her fellow students reported that a spontaneous halo framed her head while she spoke. Soon after, thirty-four other students also reportedly began speaking in languages no one could identify.

This curious incident is commonly viewed as the birth of the modern Pentecostal movement, which, disturbingly to some, is now the fastest-growing branch of Christianity worldwide.

A QUARTER OF CHRISTIANS

According to a Pew Research Center report in 2006 (its most recent Pentecostalism data), at least a quarter of the world's roughly two billion Christians then belonged to Pentecostal congregations.

Pew characterizes the various sects of Pentecostalism as "lively, highly personal faiths, which emphasize such spiritually renewing 'gifts of the Holy Spirit' as speaking in tongues, divine healing and prophesying." [174] More than other Christians, Pentecostals and other adherents of charismatic practices believe God personally affects human life through the power of the Holy Spirit, which is believed by the faithful to be co-equal in the Holy Trinity with God and Jesus, according to Pew, which conducts regular world-religion surveys.

Pentecostalism was a major influence on Christianity internationally in the twentieth century, and Pew reports that it is "poised to have an even greater influence" this century, especially in the southern hemisphere: Latin America, Africa, and Asia. [175]

Although statistics on Pentecostalism are hard to find, about ten million adherents are believed to practice their varied versions of Christianity in the United States today, most commonly in the Church of God in Christ (5.5 million members) and Assemblies of God (2.5 million) denominations. The Assemblies of God is the largest Pentecostal denomination globally, with an estimated twenty-five million members in 150 nations. [176]

TENS OF THOUSANDS JOIN DAILY

According to the Pulitzer Center on Crisis Reporting in the US, tens of thousands of Pentecostal Christians daily join the charismatic faith worldwide.

The proportion of charismatic Christians globally has spiked dramatically from only 6 percent in 1980, the center reported, to the roughly 25 percent today. In America alone, Pentecostalism increased from 3.98 percent of Christians in 1970 to 12.63 percent in 2010, and the proportion is projected to reach 20 percent by 2050, according to the center's *Pentecostal Growth Atlas*. The faith grew steadily throughout the twentieth century, despite continuous rejection by mainstream denominations and evangelical organizations, who viewed claims of faith healing and "speaking in tongues" (a.k.a., *glossalia*) as heretical and off-putting. [177]

The compelling nature of Pentecostal practices has proved seductive to many Christians, Protestant and Catholic alike. The worship of Pentecostals and to a lesser degree Charismatics is characterized by fervid emotional abandon, and because it emerged in Kansas, it's a thoroughly American creation.

"This success with mainstream Protestants and Roman Catholics in the 1970s was one of the more important events in Pentecostal history," wrote John Gordon Melton in *Encyclopaedia Britannica*, "and led to the formation of Charismatic (from Greek *charis*, "gift") fellowships in most of the major American denominations."[178]

However, many mainstream pastors viewed charismatic practices as disruptive, causing Pentecostal-leaning members to leave and form new, more-charismatic denominations.

NOT JUST PENTECOSTALS

The extraordinary emotionalism of charismatic faiths is often even evident in more mainstream churches, not only in America but worldwide.

For example, although the Russian Orthodox faith is not a Pentecostal sect, its adherents are still prone to remarkable emotional response to spiritual stimuli. When a purported piece of Saint Nicholas' rib arrived in Moscow in May 2017, the relic attracted more than a million fervent Orthodox believers. Lines reportedly stretched up to five miles from Christ the Savior Cathedral and its iconic onion-shaped dome, and the faithful waited up to ten hours to view the bone and kiss its container.

Although the church had been destroyed by the officially atheist Communist Soviets in 1931, it was rebuilt when the proportion of admitted Orthodox adherents among Russians apparently doubled to 70 percent after the Soviet Union imploded in 1991. The Saint Nicholas' rib incident was hardly the first expression of such devotion; in 2011, three million Russians viewed a belt once reputedly belonging to the Virgin Mary.[179]

The same type of emotional power led to unfettered global proliferation of Pentecostal churches, which resulted in internal efforts to orchestrate growth, resolve disagreements within the movement, and heal rifts. This began with the first Pentecostal World Conference, held in Zurich, Switzerland, in 1947, which resulted in a similar meeting the next year in the US and founding of the Pentecostal Fellowship of North America (PFNA).

Initially limited mainly to white Pentecostal churches, PFNA later reached out to include the African American Pentecostal Churches organization. In 1994 PFNA was replaced with the interracial Pentecostal/Charismatic Churches of North America.

The burgeoning of Pentecostals and Christian denominations with similar behavioral cultures underscores how central emotionality has become to the popularity and perpetuation of the Christian faith throughout the world. But what makes mainstream Christian groups so wary of Pentecostalism is the same thing that seems to make it so attractive to others: unbridled emotionalism.

'BAPTISM OF THE HOLY SPIRIT'

The distinguishing characteristic of Pentecostalism and other charismatic Christian faiths is the idea that all believers should strive to attain what is called "baptism with the Holy Spirit," which evokes the story of the Spirit's biblical descent onto the first Christians in Jerusalem on the day of Pentecost (Acts of the Apostles 2–4).

A precursor of Pentecostalism was nineteenth century's Methodism's concept of a "second work of grace," in which the faithful could spontaneously experience a transformative interaction with God. It was known as the Holiness Movement. This was different from traditional notions in which Christians received baptism of the Holy Spirit mainly through conversion or holy rites, such as baptism with water. Modern charismatics, though, believe that such random divine contact and spiritual transformation can be obtained through a process similar to Methodism founder John Wesley's "second work."

This purported interaction with the divine, where adherents "speak in tongues" and spontaneously express deep spiritual emotions, gives Pentecostal-style worship its distinctive emotive qualities. Contact with the Holy Spirit is also believed by the faithful to sometimes give those who experience it the ability to heal physical and emotional disease by laying their hands on the heads of sufferers.

This alleged supernaturally induced ability has led to many major abuses, particularly in America.

You may recall Jim Jones, pastor of the charismatic and controversial Christian People's Temple cult in San Francisco. Jones, who congregation members believed had the power to heal with his hands, relocated his flock to a wilderness in Guyana, South America, when he believed municipal authorities were persecuting the group. Traveling to Jones' Jonestown compound to investigate complaints of abuse and involuntary detention, California Congressman Leo Ryan found a fervent cult led by a seemingly paranoid, delusional Jones.

Ryan was murdered at the airport by Jones' men the day the congressman was leaving, along with three journalists; nine others were wounded. Later that day, Jones orchestrated the mass murder-suicide (those resisting were killed) of 909 inhabitants of Jonestown, including some three hundred children. Jones also died, shot by a subordinate.

Despite the manifest private experiences of joy and deliverance that charismatic beliefs seem to unleash, such assumptions can also surely lead to unspeakable tragedy, as in Guyana. When human beings are unverifiably assumed to embody supernaturally ordained powers, terrible things can follow.

The rapid growth of Pentecostalism, the most impassioned of Christian faiths, should serve as a cautionary tale that its purported gifts of emotional transcendence can also be its terrifying weakness.

"[S]ociety evolves."

— **Lori DeBlois ,**
a spokeswoman for Manhattan's trendy millennial-friendly
Soho Grand Hotel, explaining why the hotel hasn't put
Bibles in its rooms since it opened in the late 1990s [180]

CHAPTER 17

MISSING HOTEL BIBLES

A sign that American Christianity's mojo is waning

THE HUMBLE HOTEL nightstand could be viewed as a canary in the coal mine of fading religiosity in America.

Whereas 95 percent of US hotels still voluntarily placed religious materials in their rooms in 2006 (a Bible in one nightstand per room), that proportion had halved to 48 percent by 2016, according to a hotel analytics survey reported by the *Los Angeles Times*.[181]

It's relevant to note then that when Marriott International, the Mormon-owned world's largest hotel company, opened the ultra-trendy Moxy Hotel in San Diego in 2017, it placed *zero* religious material in its rooms. This is particularly interesting because Marriott still faithfully places both a Bible and Book of Mormon in other hotel rooms of its sprawling chain.

Even further ahead of the trend was New York City's hip Soho Grand Hotel. That hotel hasn't placed Bibles in its rooms since opening day in 1996.

This of course begs the question: Why the change?

Like the Soho Grand, the Moxy caters to millennials (a.k.a. "Generation Y"), young people born roughly between the early 1980s and early 2000s. Surveys reveal that Gen-Y folks are among the least religious Americans, the newest in a burgeoning demographic known as "nones" (I mentioned them previously)—atheists, agnostics and those unaffiliated with any religion—who now comprise a large and growing segment of the US population.

Bibles in US hotel rooms and elsewhere globally have long been placed free of charge by Gideons International, an organization of Protestant and Evangelical Christians founded in 1898 by two traveling businessmen who, because of overbooking at the hotel in Boscobel, Wisconsin, needed to share a room one night and got to talking.

In 1908, Gideons launched a project to place Bibles in every hotel room in America, and soon after the first such Bible appeared in a hotel in Montana. Today the organization operates in two hundred countries and distributes Bibles in more than ninety languages. In total, the organization claims it has distributed about two billion Bibles throughout the world.

But demand appears to be slowing.

"[T]he value of teaching philosophy to adolescent students is that it can stimulate the sometimes staggering discovery that there really are many different, defensible answers to many different, important, intelligible questions."

— **"The Teaching of Philosophy in American High Schools"** (1958–59), from *Proceedings and Addresses of the American Philosophical Association*[182]

CHAPTER 18

RESURRECTING SOCRATES

Why did philosophy disappear from American schools?

A
T SOME INDEFINABLE point in the murky past, those who determine what subjects American school kids are taught decided that once-essential philosophy shouldn't be one of them.

The "classics"—largely the study of ancient Mediterranean Greek and Roman philosophy and the literature and art that contains it—were once a core part of American schooling. The discipline was taught even when the new nation was being formed by Jefferson, Adams, Madison, and other classically well-educated Founding Fathers. Yet, today, philosophy is confined almost exclusively to college and university curricula. These subjects are virtually *nonexistent* in American elementary and secondary schools.

This is a big problem for the survival of reason. And for our secular republic.

THE COMMITTEE OF TEN

United States educators from the nineteenth to mid-twentieth centuries largely ignored the fact that classical philosophy, as the bedrock of Western Civilization, should have been an indispensable subject for students throughout primary and secondary schooling.

But there was one missed window of opportunity at the end of the nineteenth century, when a blue-chip group of American educators convened as The Committee of Ten to reassess and standardize the nation's pre-college education system. One of the ten, William Harris (1835–1909), the US commissioner of education from 1889 to 1906, was actually—ironically, it turned out—a world-class philosopher who had founded the well-regarded *Journal of Speculative Philosophy*.

Nonetheless, the committee ended up recommending a largely philosophy-free liberal-arts education curricula for the nation. While the proposal was generally geared to students not contemplating college study, the same curricula would be shared by all US elementary and secondary students as well, including those college-bound. The final, agreed-upon general curricula included the study of classical Greek and Latin *languages* but not classical Greek or Roman philosophy—which arguably are the crowning glories of those languages and seminal to Western civilization.

The Committee ultimately decided that because only a tiny proportion of secondary students at the time attended college thereafter, the focus of high school education should be on those who did not plan on attending a post-secondary institution. Whereas only some in the committee believed only four years of secondary school was adequate to prepare students for the "duties of life," the panel retained the four-year status quo for high school, which necessarily constricted time tightly for various areas of scholarship deemed significant. Some academic subjects were thus weeded out.

"The secondary schools of the United States, taken as a whole, do not exist for the purpose of preparing boys and girls for colleges," the Committee's final report concluded. "Only an insignificant percentage of the graduates of these schools go to colleges or scientific schools. Their main function is to prepare [students] for the duties of life…. The preparation of a few pupils for college or scientific school in the ordinary secondary school should be the incidental, and not the principal object."[183]

The committee consensus was that students could still absorb knowledge incidentally about subjects such as philosophy and deductive reasoning "through the reading and writing required of pupils or recommended to them."

Committee member James H. Baker, president of the University of Colorado, Boulder, wrote a baneful addendum to the report, explaining his deep wariness of the panel's general educational philosophy. He wrote that the conclusions:

Appear to sanction the idea that the choice of subjects in secondary schools may be a matter of comparative indifference.... All the statements are based upon the theory that, for the purposes of a general education, one study is as good as another—a theory which appears to me to ignore Philosophy, Psychology and Science of Education. It is a theory which makes education formal, and does not consider the nature and value of the content.... Secondary school programmes can not well omit mathematics, or science, or history, or the culture of the ancient classics.[184]

Baker added, importantly, that how empirical knowledge is utilized afterward is as important as how it is initially learned:

The training of 'observation, memory, expression and reasoning' (inductive) is a very important part of education, but is not all of education. The imagination, deductive reasoning, the rich possibilities of emotional life, the education of the will through ethical ideas and correct habit, all are to be considered in a scheme of learning. Ideals are to be added to the scientific method.

So, purposeful teaching of the critical-thinking skills embedded in classical philosophy thus fell dormant for a time in US primary and secondary education.

Twenty-five years later, in 1918, the National Education Association's

Commission on the Reorganization of Secondary Education created a list of educational objectives known as *The Cardinal Principles of Secondary Education*, which is to say "high school" education. The commission collaborated in a way similar to the Committee of Ten but concluded a far different paradigm shift. Commissioners decided that the nation's high school curricula should offer a flexible, buffet-style curricula to accommodate students bound for college—as the Ten had previously recommended but not enacted.

But they also recommended separate coursework more apt for less-academic students bound for somewhere else. Again, neither curricula contained once-standard philosophy instruction.

PHILOSOPHY, OR NOT

Then, in the mid-twentieth century, the American Philosophical Association (APA) sponsored yet another august gathering of educators, philosophers, administrators, and others. This group produced a 1958 report titled "The Teaching of Philosophy in American High Schools," published in its *Proceedings and Addresses of the American Philosophical Association*.

The gathered dignitaries ultimately decided that the topic was so complex and daunting they were hesitant to formally recommend a common national philosophy curriculum for all students. Instead, they just offered a neutral advisory list of pros and cons of teaching philosophy in high school, letting states and local school districts make final decisions individually about whether to offer the classics and, if so, in what form. Without a clear federal mandate, virtually all school districts chose *not* to teach philosophy, a discipline educationally challenging to both teachers and students, and one that often triggers parental fears over religious concerns.

The APA committee's "con" list, by itself, revealingly explains why philosophy still remains an outlier in American K–12 education in the twenty-first century. Although the committee's arguments in favor of teaching philosophy in US high schools were irreproachably compelling, they were apparently more than offset in their minds by the disruptive and broad emotional disquiet anticipated by the "against" list. The dominating factor was the committee's apprehension that the tenets of philosophy would be viewed by many as a challenge to Christian religious tradition.

The committee stressed that philosophy was "intrinsically valuable" and that teaching it at the secondary level would promote essential critical thinking and analysis in students. Even more important than the academic content of philosophy, the committee emphasized, was the "discipline of the mind" it engendered. The committee also noted philosophical thinking would help students become better, more thoughtful citizens and adults, and that it would protect students from intellectual vulnerability to "half-truths and dogmatic ideologies." Added to the benefits list, the committee stressed, such study would raise the bar intellectually to "bring some scholarly credibility back to teaching high school."

The main negative arguments were that high school students were too immature to understand the discipline and too closely tied to their parents' worldviews (especially regarding religion) to emotionally reconcile stark challenges to their preconceived notions that independent philosophizing might unleash.

The committee also worried that parents themselves might be unnerved that their children would be exposed to philosophical topics such as skepticism, atheism and "moral relativism," which might question the religious instruction their children were receiving.[185]

RIGHTS OF THE CHILD

This kind of conservative religious apprehension reportedly was also the main factor in the United States' singular refusal to sign the United Nations Convention on the Rights of the Child (UNCRC), ratified in 1989 by all 196 UN member states (except the US), and which took effect the next year.

The Convention holds that children individually have the right to think and believe what they want, including religious faith and practice, although under UNCRC rules parents are ostensibly allowed to non-coercively guide them.

American conservative opposition to the Convention claimed it usurped the constitutional right of parents to fully control the religious beliefs and educational curricula of their children, a particular worry of those US parents who home-schooled their children. Arch-conservative North Carolina Senator Jesse Helms at the time called UNCRC a "can of worms." It was a clear demonstration of how the embedding and perpetuation of religion is aided by limiting personal freedom and the free dispersal of substantive information, especially among children.

Blogger Anais Chartschenko, who was home-schooled as a child in her American Christian fundamentalist family, wrote that she discovered to her shame and dismay that her home-school diploma (printed by her mother) was illegitimate for college admission, and that the knowledge she had gained would be completely inadequate anyway.[186]

"Why do we allow someone to control a child's education simply because they could procreate?" she wrote in a 2013 blog post. It was the result of reason purposely hidden from faith. Chartschenko wrote that with her fundamentalist home-schooling community, the "number one goal" of education was "repression of knowledge."[187]

An excellent, best-selling 2018 memoir—*An Education*, by Tara Westover—also offers fascinating insight into the debilitating educational downsides of home-schooling in fundamentalist communities.[188]

The net result of many decades of ambivalence among American educators, politicians, and parents regarding the wisdom of teaching the "love of wisdom" is that although philosophy is routinely taught in secondary schools in Europe, Latin America, Africa, Australia, and other parts of the modern world, it is not a required K–12 subject in US schools. Indeed it is rarely taught anywhere in any form whatsoever in those grades, except indirectly as fleeting, oversimplified references to its history and content in textbooks. Which is to say, somewhat uselessly.

P4C

While there is no groundswell emerging today to return philosophy to American schools' curricula, a strong initiative is in progress to improve *how* the discipline might be better taught in the US and around the world—especially to the youngest students. It is the teaching of what Australian philosopher Paul Rudd describes as the "hinges or links of reasoning processes."

This new paradigm in pre-college philosophical teaching derives from several complementary strains of thinking that emerged in the last half of the last century—"collaborative philosophical inquiry" (CPI), "communities of inquiry," and Philosophy for Children (P4C). They largely stem from a pragmatic educational approach pioneered by John Dewey in the 1930s and Matthew Lipman (who originated P4C) early in the new millennia. Dewey and Lipman favored problem-solving exercises—"learning to think," rather than rote ingestion of facts—and the use of evidence, not emotion, to move beyond doubt to belief.

Lipman launched the P4C movement after noting with alarm when teaching undergrad philosophy at Columbia in the 1960s that his college-age students were grossly ill-equipped to reason soundly—when they should have previously acquired such skills far earlier in their lives. But the movement took a while to catch on.

Paris-based UNESCO, the UN Educational, Scientific and Cultural Organization, noted in 2007 that the practice of philosophical inquiry with children had blossomed in recent decades into a global movement represented in every region and continent. The International Council for Philosophical Inquiry with Children (ICPIC) had been founded in 1985.

In 1995 UNESCO's Paris Declaration for Philosophy asserted that "by training free, reflective minds capable of resisting various forms of propaganda, fanaticism, exclusion, and intolerance, philosophical education contributes to peace and prepares everyone to shoulder responsibilities in the face of the great challenges of the contemporary world, particularly in the field of ethics." UNESCO in 2007 also noted that philosophy would help confer in students "the necessary mental and collaborative skills necessary to thrive in a knowledge economy."[189] In 2009, that UN agency strongly recommended incorporating CPI in many Asian and Pacific countries.

Singapore later instituted in its education system a fourth "R" (after reading, writing, and arithmetic)—*reasoning*—to be taught via CPI. In Australia, philosophy is now an integral part of secondary schooling, as it is in many other countries. Nowhere does it robustly exist in US secondary education.

Now independent, the US-based nonprofit Philosophy Learning and Teaching Organization (PLATO) was established in 2009 by the American Philosophical Association to support the teaching of philosophy in K–12 grades. It promotes rigorous instruction to children, particularly before high school, in philosophy—an enriching "key, yet overlooked, resource… [that] is eminently practical." Training in the discipline is absolutely necessary to succeed in the complex, confusing twenty-first-century world where "responsible, reflective, systematic thinkers" will most likely best thrive, PLATO contends. PLATO stresses that philosophy doesn't just teach kids to answer questions but to "question answers" in discerning truth.

Yet PLATO appears to spend its energy almost exclusively on promoting *ways* of teaching philosophy, not how to insert the discipline in American K–12 school curricula in the first place.

Other underlying structural problems also remain in American education.

'MEDIA MISCOMMUNICATION'

For example, the United States' august National Science Foundation (NSF) was greatly alarmed by a 2009 Harris Poll showing more Americans believed in invisible beings than evolution, and the NSF feared America's education system was inadvertently complicit. The NSF then conducted its own survey, concluding also that "the media's miscommunication of science and the scientific process" might be helping perpetuate such beliefs.

It also turned out that US science students were generally taught by rote *what* to think, not *how*, meaning not critically, scientifically.[190] In other words, students weren't being taught to think philosophically. Most students in America are never taught that rational skepticism is a useful, protective skill, so students mostly never develop it, as university professors to their dismay have long noted.

In America, in fact, the constitutional prohibition against promoting religion in our lower schools, coupled with the lack of instruction in classical philosophy, has had the possibly unintended consequence of helping perpetuate Christianity in the United States. While kids are still getting plenty of overt Christian indoctrination *outside* school and subliminally inside with religion-heavy history texts (and after-class Bible clubs at school), they're not being introduced anywhere to classical skepticism.

It's a precarious deficit that encourages thinking that is superstitious rather than evidence-based. In effect, as Americans, we are mostly taught to indulge our innate, subconscious prejudices, which encourages us to preserve our existing belief-dependent biases, not challenge them.

So, that's where we are now in America regarding philosophy. More energy is being expended on how best one might teach it than on how to get it back into our K–12 schools, while we continue trying to protect settled science from outside distortion, mainly from religion. But the enthusiasm for P4C and collaborative philosophical inquiry is heartening nonetheless.

It's an enthralling journey we humans have traveled to so-called modernity, where today we can slip the bonds of Earth and actually transport ourselves to alien worlds and cosmic wildernesses far beyond all present knowledge—thanks to ancient philosophy. Yet we remain pathologically incapable of escaping the alluring siren songs of primeval superstitions deeply and heretofore unreachably embedded in our brains.

PART V

MOVING ON:
A PROPOSAL

AMERICA—WHICH HAS BEEN termed "the world's first secular republic"[191]—today is ironically ruled from sea to shining sea by Christianity, for reasons that most of us never even obliquely contemplate. It just *is*, affecting us and everything around us, directly and indirectly. Like air.

It wasn't actually supposed to be this way, as I discussed previously.

Thomas Jefferson, who considered any supernatural ideology an affront, wrote in an 1821 letter to his friend and rival John Adams that he yearned for a time when the human mind would retrieve "the freedom it enjoyed 2,000 years ago."[192] He was referring to the revolutionary skeptical spirit of ancient Greek philosophers that reigned before the advent Jesus, not to the pronouncements credited to the Christian prophet, although he admired the kindly sensibilities attributed to Jesus in the New Testament.

Skeptics old and new agreed with Jefferson to be very wary of established religions. Late atheist gadfly Christopher Hitchens noted that America's

Founding Fathers were Enlightenment men "who quite understood that religion could be (in the words of William Blake) a 'mind-forg'd manacle.'"[193] Even Roman poet Titus Lucretius Carus, who wrote in the last century before Christ and channeled happiness-focused Greek philosopher Epicurus, viewed mankind as, "Crushed 'neath the ponderous load of Religion's cruel burdensome shackles."[194]

Such is the venerable history of profound spiritual skepticism, leading from ancient philosophers to modern America.

The question now is how to limit the constraining effects on American progress of a religious tradition that wields an enormously outsized, in some ways monopolistic, dominance over the life of the nation.

TEACH YOUR CHILDREN WELL

There are compelling remedies but no easy ones, because they all would ultimately involve changing traditional public assumptions and habits. They also would involve formally teaching children what most of their mostly Christian parents would likely loathe them even introduced to, much less potentially seduced by: the ruthlessly questioning ethos of critical philosophy.

Given our government's role as the often-inadvertent handmaiden of Christian bias, moderating the faith's ubiquitous influence in America could be particularly challenging.

In a system such as ours, in which the Founders believed church and state should be fundamentally separate, religion in all its forms and expressions arguably should be precluded from all government-sanctioned activities and events (federal and state). Certainly, it should be prohibited from Congress. But, as we've seen, it isn't; overt sectarian religious expression in such official public contexts—necessarily mostly Christian expression due to our Christian majority—is divisive and marginalizing to out-groups. Clearly, too, such explicit public Christianity is contrary to the spirit of the Constitution's implicit church-state divide and the intent of its creators.

As I've noted before, the insidious omnipresence of Christian ideas in America is particularly impactful on children. Because of this, American kids' religions are really not their own—as religion is imparted from without, not born within. Children thus don't acquire religion privately by mature thought but have faiths handed to them by their parents, and then reinforced with indoctrination and church ritual and activities throughout childhood. It is an enforced, not voluntary, process.

Defenders of children's rights have long lamented the oppressive, unilateral way most kids are raised, particularly regarding religion. English psychologist and author Nicholas Humprey (b. 1942), who has studied human intelligence and consciousness, argues that children "have a human right not to have their minds crippled by exposure to other people's bad ideas," and that they should be free to reject their parents' religious views.

It is a distortion to present children with only one version of reality as a roadmap to their futures and their understanding of existence, especially if the demonstrable truth of their inherited version is far from settled and may very well be pure delusion. Who can say for sure whether there's a God in heaven or not? A belief, even if shared by billions of adherents, or trillions, is not confirmation that what is believed is true. It only confirms that many believe it.

Yet, children in our country learn that the belief itself is the reality. That the medium—unquestioned religion—is the message. They learn it from their parents, their churches, their schools, in the streets. They innocently absorb it from the invisible, worshipful ether wafting all about us.

CORROSIVE RELIGION

Social critics have long lamented the corrosive effect of societies' unexamined cultural traditions—e.g., Christianity in America—on children.

"I view it as one of the greatest crimes to shadow the minds of the young with these gloomy superstitions, and with fears of the unknown and the unknowable to poison all their joy in life," pivotal American suffragist and social activist Elizabeth Cady Stanton (1850–1902) once wrote.

British philosopher A.C. Grayling (b. 1949) contends that religions perpetuate because they "brainwash the young." He charges in *Against All Gods* that, "Inculcating the various competing—*competing*, note—falsehoods of the major faiths into small children is a form of child abuse, and it's a scandal."

In the United States, all of this childhood religious programming, begun in earnest in pre-school "Sunday schools," homes and via unsubstantiated assumptions oft expressed throughout the wider society, are ultimately fully embedded in the minds of young students at schools, where Christianity is unchallenged and few, if any, alternative options are offered or fully fleshed out.

Considering that countries with majority Christian populations have historically maintained their dominance over long generations, particularly in Europe and the US, it is reasonable to assume that it takes a rare independent young thinker to reject the psychological effects of such constant conditioning and not carry those biases into adulthood.

THE SECULAR MILLENNIALS

That paradigm seems to have begun to change in the past few decades, led by marked religious skepticism in younger demographics, and it is manifestly a global trend.

According to a 2018 Pew Research Center report on religious attitudes in more than one hundred countries, adults under forty years of age in forty-six countries, including the US, "are less likely to say religion is 'very important' in their lives." The opposite is true in only two countries (Georgia and Ghana), whereas in fifty-eight countries no significant age gap in belief was found. Religious doubt has been trending upward for some time in America, as younger citizens in particular show themselves to be less likely than older people to attend church, believe in God, or describe religion as important to them.[195]

In 2018, 43 percent of under-forty Americans claimed religion was important to them, whereas 60 percent of older adults did. A *New York Times* story in 2015 noted that, "A remarkable 25 percent of Americans born after 1980, the group often known as millennials, are not religious, compared with 11 percent of baby boomers and 7 percent of the generation born between 1928 and 1945."[196]

Although proposed reasons for spiritual slippage among the young are not definitive, the 2018 Pew report speculated that increasing education opportunities might be a factor because they are usually inversely proportionate to intensity of religious faith. Another theory considers that as countries flourish economically their inhabitants focus less on survival and a possible hereafter and more on maximizing benefits in the here and now.

"According to this line of thinking, each generation in a steadily developing society would be less religious than the last, which would explain why young adults are less religious than their elders at any given time," Pew reported.[197]

Michael Hout, a sociology professor at New York University, theorizes that US millennials grew up with "baby boomer" parents who told their children it was "important to think for themselves—that they find their own moral compass," rejecting the traditional idea that a good kid was an obedient one.

"That's at odds with organizations, like churches, that have a long tradition of official teaching and obedience," Hout told Pew. "And more than any other group, millennials have been and are still being formed in this cultural context. As a result, they are more likely to have a 'do-it-yourself' attitude toward religion."[198]

Yet, a majority of Americans, millennials or otherwise, are still religious, and the indoctrination of children in religious ideas continues unabated.

RELIGION = SUPERSTITION

Modern American public schools, of course, are constitutionally prohibited from religious proselytizing, but their textbooks teach the centrality of Christianity in Western history without ever describing or identifying Christianity for what, *by definition*, it inarguably is: *superstition*. It's a spectacularly successful superstition, to be sure, surviving, even strengthening over millennia and today informing much about the greatest superpower the world has ever known. But superstition it is, nevertheless, as much as voodoo curses, alien abductions and ill-omened black cats.

Nonetheless, Christians I know adamantly reject the proposition that Christianity is fundamentally superstitious, viewing the term as wholly unjustified in the context of their faith. But all supernatural religions, including

Christianity, are, indeed, *definitively* superstitious, according to prominent mainstream dictionaries, such as Merriam-Webster, whose definition of "superstition' is:

> *1a: a belief or practice resulting from ignorance, fear of the unknown, trust in magic or chance, or a false conception of causation.*

> *1b: an irrational abject attitude of mind toward the supernatural, nature or God resulting from superstition.*

> *2: a notion maintained despite evidence to the contrary.*

The online Oxford Dictionary's definition is:

> *1: excessively credulous belief in and reverence for supernatural beings. "He dismissed the ghost stories as mere superstition" Synonyms: unfounded, credulity, magic, sorcery, witchcraft, fallacy, delusion, illusion, unfounded belief. Antonyms: science.*

Each of these definitions directly pertains to Christianity and all other supernatural religious beliefs, which exist despite much "evidence to the contrary," considering that purported supernatural beings and events have never been undeniably produced, or reproduced, in reality.

Yet, Christianity's unverified doctrines and attitudes still dominate American culture.

Scholars I know have recommended that I suspend defining supernatural religion as superstition until after consulting the writings of eminent Christian philosophers like Alvin Plantinga, Eleonor Stump, William Lane Craig, Ed Feser, Peter Kreeft, and others. However, even they would have to arbitrarily change the standard definition of "superstition" to make a convincing case.

SCHOOL DAZE

This glaring lack of confirmation for Christianity's dogmas regarding the creation of the universe has not stopped proponents from actively trying to insinuate religious ideas—e.g., Bible-based "Creationism" and pseudo climate concepts—into American school curricula to dilute instruction in established scientific principles. The net result is that evolution and other scripture-debunking science are far-too-fractionally taught in American public schools (forget about religious schools).

It's not a new worry. "Those who would legislate against the teaching of evolution should also legislate against gravity, electricity and the unreasonable velocity of light," American botanist Luther Burbank (1849–1926) once satirically suggested. He sarcastically added that a clause should also prohibit telescopes, microscopes and spectroscopes, or any future precision tool that might "be invented, constructed or used for the discovery of truth."

This is just as Marin Luther proclaimed centuries earlier without a hint of sarcasm. Reason, he said, was the "greatest whore."

The problem in the twenty-first century is, "There are a lot of legislators who are afraid that kids will learn science and lose their faith," and who are more than willing to pass such laws, Arizona State University physics professor Lawrence Krauss worries. Such thinking has successfully kept a lot of essential knowledge and critical thinking out of our public-school curricula.

Thus, today's American school children go through their elementary and secondary school years with constant but unsubstantiated reaffirmation that the core beliefs of Christianity are reality-based and substantive, much like the principles of democracy or mathematics.

In their classes, they learn virtually nothing to counter that. Impressionable students are never taught that Western civilization has been built almost completely on the tension and interplay—the war, arguably—between the ethereal, superstitious claims of Christianity and the often godless, down-to-earth, naturalist claims of the ancient Greek philosophers.

Today's students also don't learn that countless very smart, reasonable people have believed throughout history that Christianity's central claims (i.e., God originally created human beings exactly as they appear today) are not only unprovable but *provably* false. Or that serious doubters fearful of public persecution or rejection by majority believers—Copernicus and Darwin, to name two—have often, if not always, disingenuously parsed, far understated or even hidden the depth of their religious skepticism and unbelief all their lives. Even when they were undeniably correct. *Especially* when correct.

Without the ballast of competing facts, this has left the default but fictitious impression among billions of people that Christian notions are incontrovertibly valid and that the faithful should always remain very wary of any claims to the contrary. Especially children.

THINKING CRITICALLY

To more fully understand how our world and species *actually* came to exist and gradually develop over unimaginably long spans of time, our children profoundly need to learn about both core explanatory traditions—one where humankind and the cosmos purportedly arose from divine fiat, and the other, from the universal, material laws of nature.

Students also need to learn how to critically think about both to determine which is more plausible and demonstrable, with the same methodical analysis they should apply to every such question. This rigorous critical process will not guarantee a reasonable outcome, but it has a far better chance than unquestioning acceptance of supernatural faith.

Certainly, a bright, curious student armed with the curious ethos of rational materialism might end up seriously doubting everything unsupported by reality. Indeed, that student might become particularly suspicious of any supernatural explanation that seeks to kill doubt and analysis. But intelligent curiosity and skepticism are not, by themselves, a cure-all for ignorance and misunderstanding. When it comes to accurately perceiving reality, our genes and brains appear to routinely deceive us. Part of education should be learning to differentiate between reconfirmable knowledge in the material world and deep-seated, biased intuition from an absent ether.

Certain human psychological propensities ensure that even wholly unsubstantiated religious beliefs "may be sustained in spite of the improbability of the theological representations," British zoologist Robert Hinde warned in *Why Gods Persist*. [199] In other words, evolution seems to have designed us to ignore irrefutable reality far too easily and often.

For many understandable reasons, as I've described, Christianity has come to completely dominate our society, while rational materialism—except in science—has become mostly invisible, especially to children. The result is that, generation after generation after generation, Christianity is perpetuated, partly because children are fully and continuously indoctrinated in religious faith while not given full, unedited, undiluted knowledge about the manifest actualities of the real world. Therefore, most Americans grow up intellectually stunted, armed with a divine *sense* that has been densely layering in human genes and memes for eons, and further enhanced by a culturally imposed bias favoring invisible deities.

But what most undermines our children's (and our own) rationality is also built-in: a powerful, genetically endowed defensive urge to attack *anything* that appears to question our faiths. Before even thinking about it. This relates to a key insight of modern neuroscience, according to an article in *Mother Jones* magazine:

> *Reasoning is actually suffused with emotion (or what researchers often call "affect"). Not only are the two inseparable, but our positive or negative feelings about people, things, and ideas arise much more rapidly than our conscious thoughts, in a matter of milliseconds—fast enough to detect with an EEG device, but long before we're aware of it. That shouldn't be surprising: Evolution required us to react very quickly to stimuli in our environment. It's a "basic human survival skill," explains political scientist Arthur Lupia of the University of Michigan. We push threatening information away; we pull friendly information close. We apply fight-or-flight reflexes not only to predators, but to data itself.[200]*

This is how human beings, often wrongheadedly, respond to new information that contradicts what we already believe.

A paragraph on *The Skeptics Dictionary* website very lucidly explains what this bias is and how it operates:

Motivated reasoning is confirmation bias taken to the next level. Motivated reasoning leads people to confirm what they already believe, while ignoring contrary data. But it also drives people to develop elaborate rationalizations to justify holding beliefs that logic and evidence have shown to be wrong. Motivated reasoning responds defensively to contrary evidence, actively discrediting such evidence or its source without logical or evidentiary justification. Clearly, motivated reasoning is emotion driven. It seems to be assumed by social scientists that motivated reasoning is driven by a desire to avoid cognitive dissonance. Self-delusion, in other words, feels good, and that's what motivates people to vehemently defend obvious falsehoods.[201]

Even as they near adulthood, American youths are further shielded from ideas that might threaten their fundamental values, attitudes, and assumptions. Mollycoddling of students' sensibilities with excessive "safe spaces" and overly vigorous policing of "microaggressions" at US colleges and universities, for example, shield students from being confronted with opposing viewpoints that might directly reject their own deepest beliefs. That is exactly what a good education *mustn't* do.

Daniel W. Drezner, a Tufts University international politics professor and Brookings Institution fellow, wrote in a *Washington Post* article that on the first day of class every semester he tells his students that, "If your core beliefs haven't been challenged at least once during your time here, then you're not doing it right."[202]

Exactly. Critical thinking, correctly applied, should deeply challenge students. That's when real learning and intellectual growth take place, during conscientious separation of wheat from chaff. However, this also must be leavened, of course, by a reasonable awareness and sensitivity to the reality that many students must deal with significant past personal trauma (e.g., sexual assault and racial animus), which is the proximate goal of safe spaces.

However, by too aggressively shielding our children from such essential opportunities for critical development, especially self-challenging ones, we also shield them from reality. And we perpetuate preposterous thinking, including the apparently innate but clearly cultivated tendency to presume things exist that almost certainly don't.

Despite the yawning crevasse that separates natural versus supernatural understandings of the world, compelling explanations do exist in material reality. In the hardness of a stone, the invisible pull of gravity, the visceral urge to love. Maybe not the overarching answer to everything, but incremental answers that, as science demonstrates, can lead step by step toward larger truths.

But without freewheeling critical thinking that does not arbitrarily protect certain ideas from rigorous skeptical analysis—e.g., concepts of divinity—the quest for answers, for material truth, is dangerously constrained and retarded.

REINCARNATING PHILOSOPHY

Such is the case in America today, because the root discipline of critical thinking, classical Greek philosophy—the ancient field of learning that ultimately spawned science—is not methodically taught in our elementary or high schools. It's also not publicly exalted in our culture the way religion or even science is, and hasn't piggy-backed on our DNA down countless millennia with the same power and tenacity that emotional religiosity has.

So, practically speaking, students should start learning early the most rational tools of philosophy—particularly serious critical-thinking skills— *before* all their core attitudes and unquestioned beliefs are fully established in their minds. Before their ability to reasonably analyze unfamiliar, even contrary, concepts is permanently compromised. Before they are unable, as Aristotle said of an educated mind, to "entertain a thought without accepting it."

An effective education should teach children to *not* always blindly, thoughtlessly accept what people tell them, including their parents. But to require sensible evidence. Kids already do this naturally with parents (as every parent knows), except when their resistance is summarily crushed by the imbalance of power. Less crushing might be helpful in development of your children's critical faculties.

Critical thinking is at a crossroads in America in the new millennium, as wide swathes of the population, encouraged by an aggressively anti-intellectual president, reject even the concepts of material fact and verifiable truth. Suddenly, for many, all truth is in the mind of the beholder, requiring no external corroboration. Much like Christianity, but it's real life.

Lawyer and author Michael Shammas contends that "rationality is missing" in our current politics and that philosophy offers the only bridge over the intellectual divide. Philosophical reflection, Shammas writes, "at least opens one up to the possibility that one is wrong." A person who does not understand the history of thought in Western Civilization bequeathed by the Greeks, "does not understand the rationality behind our political system," he argues.[203]

START EARLY

Although Shammas sees high school as an ideal time to start teaching philosophy, I believe elementary school is where it should begin—the earlier, the better. Those early years are when a lot of the damage is done to our children's ability to fairly analyze material reality and learn to challenge dangerous speculations.

If nothing else, philosophy classes should teach students to ruthlessly question every proposition, and demand adequate supportive material evidence. From whether $2 + 2 = 4$, to how many angels could conceivably dance on a pinhead, to the age of the Earth, to how our species biologically evolved. Everything.

I believe educating children without a thorough grounding in practical natural philosophy is a grievous insult to learning and a willful affliction of dangerous ignorance on them and, thus, on our *collective* future.

TEACH RELIGION, TOO

Perhaps paradoxically, I see value, as well, in survey teaching about the history of world religions as an important aspect of our development as a species. But only if each faith is presented equitably as historical fact and without emphasis on or bias toward any particular creed—or promoting and glorifying religion, or stipulating the veracity of its imaginings. However, such courses should be taught alongside the history of philosophical doubt, an equal if not more important factor in the development of Western civilization.

Notably, I myself didn't learn how widespread and pronounced religious skepticism was until I read about it in my sixties in a wonderful, engrossing book by historian Jennifer Michael Hecht, *Doubt: A History.*

Certainly, if students are pressed to rigorously question the putative revealed "truth" of the religion they received from their parents, they may sense a lie. But, if their religious assumptions are defensible, they will survive, as rigorously questioned but empirically sound ideas in science ultimately survive and flourish. So, while new knowledge might conceivably lead some children away from religion, it might just as well lead some back. So be it.

A FULL EDUCATION

That is my humble wish: that American children get a full education not restricted by religious apprehensions and the resulting sins of omission that have infested America's schools for 240 years—from global-warming denial to watered-down evolution science to irrational sex education to disingenuous labeling of "religion" in textbooks as somehow *not* superstition.

Let's teach young students everything essential in a fair and balanced way, withholding nothing sensible. Let's trust in their innate intelligence, hoping that with all the material knowledge we can give them in their impressionable years they will make more reasonable, rational decisions about everything throughout the rest of their lives. And that they will become more naturally kind, moral, altruistic and reasonable human beings. Even "mad" scientists, hard-core atheists and zealous rational humanists can be really good people, too, it turns out. Who knew?

WHITHER GOD?

In the fall of 2004, a mix of theologians, lay philosophers, and scholars of religion from many schools gathered at the University of Colorado, Boulder to discuss "The Hiddenness of God." According to physicist and author Victor Stenger, who attended the event, the group met solely to divine, if possible, a rational explanation for the fact that "no empirical evidence for God exists."[204]

It's the question that drove me to research and write this book, and to wonder about the purpose of life without divinity.

When asked for what purpose mankind was created, James Watson, co-discoverer (with Francis Crick) of the double-helix structure of DNA in 1953, replied in part, "I don't think it is *for* anything. We're just products of evolution. You can say, 'Gee, your life must be pretty bleak if you don't think there's a purpose.' But, I'm anticipating having a good lunch."[205]

Asked about the purpose of evolution and what it told him about God, British biologist and insect aficionado J.B.S. Haldane (1892–1964) made a gentle joke. "The Creator, if He exists, has an inordinate fondness for beetles,"[206] Haldane said playfully, noting the lowly, crawling creatures' startling ubiquity on the planet.

Evolution, the foundation of modern biology, destroys one of the oldest illusory ideas of mankind, as philosopher Daniel Dennett noted—that "it takes a big fancy smart thing to make a lesser thing. I call that the trickle-down theory of creation. You'll never see a spear making a spear maker. You'll never see a horse shoe making a blacksmith. You'll never see a pot making a potter."[207] But in evolution, of course, genes—among the tiniest, most inert fundamentals of nature—created fancy us.

Certainly, for such materialism to become mainstream would require some philosophical realignment of our traditional human paradigm, possibly permanently redefining all supernatural ideas as myth, like the realm of Zeus and Apollo, long ago relegated to historical fiction. We need to move beyond our intellectual inertia, which Richard Dawkins credits to "One of the truly bad effects of religion... that it teaches us that it is a virtue to be satisfied with not understanding."[208]

Which begins when we start indoctrinating our children in Christianity.

"Just think of the tragedy of teaching children not to doubt," said legendary defense attorney Clarence Darrow in the so-called Scopes Monkey Trial in 1925.

Indeed.

POSITIVE RELIGION

What I *don't* wish to disrespect or attack are the comforts and reassurances of anyone's private religious faith, or wish more terror or suffering in the world than there already is. I accept that human compulsion toward religious faith exists in reality, even if the only-imagined objects and realms of its adoration don't.

I just believe that separating fact from fiction is critical to an accurate understanding of our all-too-brief existence in this remote wilderness in the endless cosmos. In fact, it's very probably our *only* existence. Ever. Mortal or otherwise.

Whatever our beliefs, we need to be vigilant about what we believe and the things our beliefs compel us to do; there are mortal dangers to being unaware that our myths can seamlessly masquerade as reality. Think the Islamic State. Or the Christian Identity Movement. Or white supremacy. Or faith healing.

In any event, if we are to evolve into a more rational, less religious society, it will take time. As Freud recommended, to outgrow God in psychic comfort, people must do it at their own pace. But we should try to keep in mind that *inertia* is not a pace. However, realigning our spiritual lights appears to be doable, eventually. As Dean Hamer noted in *The God Gene,* just because genes can unleash surges of spiritual feeling in us, they don't control our destinies. "What we do with our spiritual genes," he stressed, "is very much up to us."[209]

While we may not be ready at the moment for such a major paradigm shift, however promising, we should be aware of the grave dangers in doing nothing, "The sleep of reason brings forth monsters," Francis Wheen wrote apprehensively in in *How Mumbo-Jumbo Conquered the World,* and "The proliferation of obscurantist bunkum and the assault on reason are a menace to civilization." He fears "the humane values of the enlightenment have been abandoned or betrayed."[210]

And it all begins in our youth. French existentialist Jean-Paul Sartre, in *The Flies* (1937), rails against the terrorism of religious indoctrination in childhood:

The child: I'm frightened.

The woman: And so you should be, darling. Terribly frightened. That's how one grows up into a decent, god-fearing man.[211]

This cannot be a realistic way of thinking for each of us to inherit and probably ought to be reconsidered. As German philosopher and Communism founder Karl Marx once wrote and had carved in his gravestone—and I must stress I am no Marxist but just appreciate the tenor of the quote— "Philosophers have hitherto only *interpreted* the world in various ways; the point is to *change* it."[212]

Let's start a discussion there. Should we change? And if so, how? My recommendation is to start vigorously teaching philosophy and practical critical-thinking skills to school children of every generation and hope for the best.

But let's start soon. We may have already wasted about three thousand years on mostly fuzzy thinking since the ancient Greeks. However, honestly, given the spiritual dreaminess and creative self-deception of human nature— plus our tendencies toward ruthless authoritarianism—I can't imagine how things could have turned out any other way. Especially in America.

Unless, of course, Plato never existed, Rome never rose, or fell, Constantine had been stillborn, and a boundless capacity for imagining invisible beings never evolved in the human brain.

The End

ABOUT THE AUTHOR

Born into a nominally Catholic family in 1950, author Rick Snedeker concluded by his senior year in high school that the ghostly beings and realms of all supernatural religions must be fantasies. Over the coming years, as he observed how most Americans were completely in thrall to their supernatural imaginings, the seeming irrationality of such apparent delusions increasingly mystified him.

That bewildering reality of ubiquitous faith among Americans led Snedeker to research and write this book, his second nonfiction work. *Holy Smoke* investigates how the deep embedding of Christianity in colonial America robustly perpetuated the faith into the 21st century, despite the nation's founding as a secular democracy—and how that bodes ill for American democracy.

A former newspaper and magazine journalist and public relations editor, Snedeker today writes a daily nonreligious blog, *Godzooks*, on the Patheos hub online. He also writes op-ed pieces for assorted newspapers and magazines. Although he now resides in the South Dakota, on the Great Plains of the American Midwest, New York-born Snedeker intermittently lived in Saudi Arabia for a total of 26 years, as well as in Arizona. Snedeker's memoir of his boyhood in an American oil camp in Saudi Arabia, *3,001 Arabian Days*, was published in 2018.

ENDNOTES

1   **Preface**
    (Andrew Brown, "If a former pope says non-Catholics can go to heaven, why be Catholic?" *The Guardian*, March 22, 2019, https://tinyurl.com/yxfr6vvb.)

2   (Michael W. Chapman, "The Pope: 'There is no Hell,'" *CNSnews.com*, March 29, 2018, https://tinyurl.com/yaqg5h76.)

3   (Julian Baggini, "Atheism in America," *Financial Times*, February 3, 2012, https://tinyurl.com/y6zogb3b.)

4   (Susan Du, "U of M study says we still dislike the atheists most; we're just not sure why," *City Pages*, September 20, 2016, https://tinyurl.com/y5kts2od.)

5   ("Reason is the Devil's whore," Whole Reason: Thoughtful Christianity, last updated September 27, 2010, https://tinyurl.com/y64oy7uh.)

6   (Lucien Jerphagnon and Jean Orcibal, "Blaise Pascal," Britannica.com, last updated August 15, 2018, https://www.britannica.com/biography/Blaise-Pascal.)

Introduction
7   ("U.S. Religious Landscape Survey," Pewforum.org, 2019, https://www.pewforum.org/religious-landscape-study/)

8   (Annette Gordon-Reed and Peter S. Onuf, "Thomas Jefferson's Bible Teaching," *The New York Times*, July 4, 2017, https://tinyurl.com/y3whnxc2)

9   (Christine Leigh Heyrman, "Church and State in British North America," TeacherServe, last updated January 2008, https://tinyurl.com/y6zcfmvh.)

10 ("Emerson vs Board of Education," Cornell Law School Legal Information Institute, last updated February 10, 2019, https://www.law.cornell.edu/supremecourt/text/330/1.)

11 (Noreen Malone, "Why Doesn't Every President Use the Lincoln Bible?" *Slate*, January 19, 2009, https://tinyurl.com/y2pxr9qw)

12 (Dean Hamer, *The God Gene: How Faith is Hardwired into our Genes*, Doubleday, 2004.)

13 (Chris Mooney, "The Republican Brain: The Science of Why They Deny Science and Reality," Wiley, 2012.)

14 (Kathy Lynn Grossman, "Christians drop, 'nones' soar in new religion portrait," *USA Today*, May 12, 2015, https://tinyurl.com/yy97enw3.)

Chapter 1: Contact

15 ("Roanoke Colony Deserted," This Day in History: August 18, 1590, 2017, https://tinyurl.com/myvdunc.)

16 (Ibid.)

Chapter 2: Christianity Arrives in America

17 ("Pilgrim Fathers," Britannica.com, last updated July 12, 2018, https://www.britannica.com/topic/Pilgrim-Fathers.)

18 ("The Mayflower Compact," Britannica.com, last updated August 4, 2011, https://www.britannica.com/topic/Mayflower-Compact.)

19 (Richard E. Pierson and Jennifer Pierson, *Pierson Millennium*, Heritage Books, 1997, 88.)

20 (Wendy Warren, *New England Bound*, Liveright, 2016, introduction.)

21 ("Primary Sources for the First Thanksgiving in Plymouth," Pilgrim Hall Museum, last updated December 13, 2012, http://www.pilgrim-hallmuseum.org/pdf/TG_What_Happened_in_1621.pdf.)

22 (John Winthrop, *Journal of John Winthrop*, eds. Dunn, Savage, Yeandle, Harvard University Press, 1996.)

Chapter 3: A 'City Upon the Hill'

23 (Julie Zauzmer, "Christians are more than twice as likely to blame a person's poverty on lack of effort," *Washington Post*, August 3, 2017, https://tinyurl.com/y43ydfnu.)

24 ("The Protestant Ethic and the Spirity of Capitalism," Sparknotes, accessed February 11, 2019, https://www.sparknotes.com/philosophy/protestantethic/summary/.)

25 (Matthew Scott Holland, *Bonds of Affection*, Georgetown University Press, 2007, 2.)

26 ("John Calvin and the Puritan Founders of New England," Chalcedon Presbyterian Church, accessed July 27, 2017, https://tinyurl.com/y38gmk3h.)

27 (David Hall, *The Legacy of John Calvin: His Influence in the Modern World*, P&R Publishing, 2008, 111.*)*

28 (McNeill, John T. McNeill, *The History and Character of Calvinism*, Oxford University Press, 1954, 335.)

Chapter 4: Babel

29 (Jon Butler, Grant Wacker and Randall Balmer, *Religion in America: A Short History*, Oxford University Press, 2011, chap. 1, Apple ebook.)

30 (Kenneth C. Davis, "America's True History of Religiouis Tolerance," Smithsonian.com, last updated October 2010, https://tinyurl.com/zl886bf.)

31 (Butler, et al, chap. 1, ibid.)

32 (Ibid.)

33 (Ibid.)

34 (Ibid.)

35 (Ibid.)

36 (Ibid.)

37 (Ibid.)

38 (Ibid.)

39 (Ibid.)

40 (Ibid.)

41 (Ibid.)

42 (Ibid.)

Chapter 5: Intolerance

43 ("Puritanism," Britannica.com, accessed July 27, 2017, https://www.britannica.com/topic/Puritanism.)

44 ("America as a Religious Refuge: The Seventeenth Century, Part 2," Library of Congress, Religion and the Founding of the American Republic, accessed July 27, 2017, http://loc.gov/exhibits/religion/rel01-2.html.)

45 (Thomas Herbert Johnson, *The Puritans: A Sourcebook of Their Writings*, Courier Corp., 2001, 185.*)*

46 (Roger Williams, *The Correspondence of Roger Williams*, University Press of New England, 1988, 12-23.)

47 (Polin and Polin, American Political Thought, 60.)

48 (Dierenfield, Bruce J. Dierenfield, "The Battle Over School Prayer: How Engel vs. Vitale Changed America," in Landmark Law Cases & American Society, University Press of Kansas, 2007, 5.)

49 ("Where Did 'Separation of Church and State Come From?" Livescience, last updated October 19, 2010, https://tinyurl.com/y5y6c9ny.)

50 (Dickinson 2005, John Dickinson, "Pennsylvania Journal May 12, 1768," in *The Founders of Religion*, Princeton University Press, 2005, 60-61.)

51 (James E. Ernst, *Roger Williams: New England Firebrand*, MacMillan, 1932, 227-28.)

52 ("Antinomian Controversy," Encyclopedia.com, last updated 2003, https://tinyurl.com/y2v298do.)

53 ("Anne Hutchinson," Britannica.com, last updated October 29, 2014, http://www.britannica.com/EBchecked/topic/277653/Anne-Hutchinson.)

54 ("People & Ideas: The Puritans," PBS, God in America, last updated October 11, 2017, http://www.pbs.org/godinamerica/people/puritans.html.)

55 ("The Settlement of Maryland (1634), History.com, last updated March 25, 2017, http://www.history.com/this-day-in-history/the-settlement-of-maryland.)

56 (James D. DiLisio, "Maryland: The Colony," Britannica.com, last updated July 20, 2014, http://www.britannica.com/EBchecked/topic/367594/Maryland/78204/The-colony.)

Chapter 6: Salem's Lot

57 (Robert Calef, *More Wonders of the Visible World*, Cushing and Appleton, 1823, 225.)

58 (Shirley Jackson, *The Witchcraft of Salem Village*, Random House, 1956, 10-12.)

59 (Jeff Wallenfeldt, "American History: Salem Witch Trials," Britannica.com, last updated March 17, 2017, https://www.britannica.com/event/Salem-witch-trials.)

60 (Megan Gannon, "A Bewitching History: Why Witches Ride Broomsticks," Livescience.com, last updated October 30, 2013, https://www.livescience.com/40828-why-witches-ride-broomsticks.html.)

61 (Stacy Shiff, "Unraveling the Many Mysteries of Tituba, the Star Witness of the Salem Witch Trials," Smithsonianmag.com, last updated November 2015, https://tinyurl.com/y6ue9bhw.)

62 (David K. Goss, *Daily Life During the Salem Witch Trials*, Greenwood Press, 2012, 217.)

63 (Jewett, Clarence F. Jewett, *The Memorial History of Boston, Including Suffolk County, Massachusetts, 1630-1880*, Ticknkor and Company, 133-37.)

64 (Lewis, Wolpert, *Six Impossible Things Before Breakfast: The Evolutionary Origins of Belief,*" Faber and Faber Ltd., 2010, chap. 9, Apple eBook.)

Chapter 7: The Great Spirit

65 ("Ghost Dance," United States History, accessed July 28, 2017, http://www.u-s-history.com/pages/h3775.html.)

66 (Vine Deloria Jr., *God is Red: A Native View of Religion*, Fulcrum Publishing, 1993, 1.)

67 ("American Indian Relilgious Freedom Act (AIRFA)," National Oceanic and Atmospheric Administration, last updated August 11, 1978, https://tinyurl.com/y6tpuz76.)

Chapter 8: Negro spiritual

68 ("Religious Landscape Study," Pewforum.com, last updated 2017, http://www.pewforum.org/religious-landscape-study/.)

69 ("Proslavery in the Early South," in *Proslavery and Sectional Thought in the Early South: 1740-1829, An Anthology*, ed. Jeffery Robert Young, University of South Carolina Press, 2006, 1.)

70 ("Exodus 21:12 20-21," Bible Hub, accessed February 25, 2019, https://biblehub.com/exodus/21-12.htm.)

71 ("Genesis 9: 20-27," Bible Gateway, accessed February 25, 2019, https://tinyurl.com/y4hbkudq.)

72 (Richard Reddie, "Atlantic Slave Trade and Abolition," BBC Online, last updated January 29, 2007, https://tinyurl.com/c94ncz.)

73 (Jon Butler, Grant Wacker and Randall Balmer, *Religion in America: A Short History*, Oxford University Press, 2011, chap. 1, Apple ebook, 4.)

74 (Mark Galli, "Defeating the Conspiracy," Christian History Institute, accessed July 27, 2017, https://www.christianhistoryinstitute.org/magazine/article/defeating-the-conspiracy/.)

75 (Lewis, Wolpert, Six Impossible Things Before Breakfast: The Evolutionary Origins of Belief," Faber and Faber Ltd., 2010, chap. 10, Apple eBook.)

76 (Galli, Ibid.)

77 (Colin A. Palmer, *Passageways: An Interpretive History of Black America, 1619-1863*, Wadsworth Group, 2002, 158.)

78 (Albert J. Raboteau, *Slave Religion: The "Invisible Institution" in the Antebellum South*, Oxford University Press, 1978 (updated 2004), 92.)

79 ("The Making of African American Identity, Vol. 1, 1500-1865," Toolbox Library: Primary Resources in U.S. History and Literature, accessed July 28, 2017, https://tinyurl.com/y3ohxvzs.)

80 (Ibid.)

81 (Galli, Ibid.)

82 (Ibid.)

83 (Frank Christopher, *Nat Turner: A Troublesome Property*, Youtube film, 2003, https://www.youtube.com/watch?v=4wzAibf06Is&t=615s.)

84 ("Nat Turner," History.com, last updated September 12, 2018, https://www.history.com/topics/black-history/nat-turner.)

85 (Galli, Ibid.)

Chapter 9: Our Wary Founders

86 (Edward L. Bond, *Damned Souls in a Tobacco Colony: Religion in Seventeenth-Century Virginia*, Mercer University Press, 2000, 130.)

87 (H.J. Eckinrode, archivist,"Separation of Church and State in Virginia: A Study in the Development of a Revolultion," University of Virginia special report, 1910, 153.)

88 (David W. Mandell, *Atheist Acromonious*, Vervante, 2008, 180.)

89 (Stephen J. Gould, "Separation of Church and State," Refusing the Notion the U.S. was Founded on Christianity, accessed February 24, 2017, http://www.stephenjaygould.org/ctrl/quotes_founders.html.)

90 (Lester J. Cappon, ed., *The Adams-Jefferson Letters: The Complete Correspondence Between Thomas Jefferson and John Adams*, University of South Carolina, 1987, 568.)

91 (John H. Rhodehamel, ed., "Letter to the members of the New Church in Baltimore, January 27, 1793," in *George Washington: Writings*, Library of Congress, 1997, 834.)

92 ("Treaty Between the United States and Tripoli, 1796," US Constitution.net, accessed February 26, 2019, https://usconstitution.net/tripoli.html.)

93 (John Adams, "A Defense of the Constitutions of Government of the United States of America, 1787-1788," in *The American Enlightenment*, ed. Adrienne Koch, George Braziller, 1965, 258.)

94 (Susan Jacoby, *Freethinkers: A History of American Secularism*, Henry Holt & Co., 2014, 13.)

95 ("James Madison, Letter to Robert Walsh, March 2, 1819," in *James Madison: Writings*, Library of America, 1999, 726-27.)

96 ("Visualize No Liberals," Freethought Almanac, last updated August 19, 2011, https://tinyurl.com/y2xa3kqs.)

Chapter 10: Revolution

97 (Cassandra Niemczyk, "Christianity and the American Revolution: Did You Know?" Christianitytoday.com, last updated 1996, https://tinyurl.com/y6f3tpqh.)

98 ("Religion and the American Revolution," *Religion and the Founding of the American Revolution*, Library of Congress, accessed July 28, 2017, https://www.loc.gov/exhibits/religion/rel03.html.)

99 ("The Church and the Revolutionary War," History Detectives: Special Investigation, PBS, 2014, https://tinyurl.com/lbn72h5.)

100 (David Hein and Gardiner H. Shattuck Jr., *The Episcopalians*, Church Publishing, 2004, 230.)

101 ("History of the American Church," The Episcopal Church, last updated 1999, https://www.episcopalchurch.org/page/history-american-church.)

102 (Ibid.)

103 (Richard Darwardine, "Methodists, Politics, and the Coming of the American Civil War," Church History, vol. 69, 2000, 578-609.)

104 (John T. McGreevy, *Catholicism and American Freedom: A History*, W.W. Norton and Co., 2004, 8.)

105 (William Byrne, "History of the Catholic Church in the New England States," Hurd & Everts Co., 1899, 97.)

106 (Butler, et al, chap. 7.)

Chapter 11: The Great Awakening

107 (Jon Butler, Grant Wacker and Randall Balmer, *Religion in America: A Short History*, Oxford University Press, 2011, chap. 9, Apple E-book.)

108 (Butler, et al., ibid.)

109 (Sydney E. Ahlstrom, *A Religious History of the American People*, Yale Univdersity Press, 1972, 283.)

110 (Kidd, The Great Awakening, 416.)

111 ("Revivalism," Britannica.com, last updated May 31, 2013, http://www. britannica.com/EBchecked/topic/500552/revivalism.)

112 (Ibid.)

113 ("1859: The Impact of the Great Awakenings — Ongoing Effects of Revival," The Third Great Awakening, last updated 2015, http://www. thegreatawakenings.org/3GA/3T1859aTheimpact.htm.)

114 (D.G. Reid, R.D. Linder, B.L. Shelley and H.S. Stout, "Cane Ridge Revival," in *Dictionary of Christianity in America,* Inter-Varsity Press, 1990, 64.)

115 (William J. Frost, "Christianity: A Social and Cultural History," *Christianity and Culture in America*, 1998, 681.)

116 (Mark Galli, "Revival at Cane Ridge," *Christian History Institute magazine*, 1995, https://tinyurl.com/y5h2tgd7.)

117 (Ibid.)

118 (Ibid.)

119 (Ibid.)

120 ("Revivalism," Britannica.com, last updated Mau 31, 2013, http://www. britannica.com/EBchecked/topic/500552/revivalism.)

121 (Mary Fairchild, "Christianity Today: General Statistics and Facts of Christianity," On Religion, last updated January 10, 2015, https:// tinyurl.com/ydtjdgp.)

122 (Ibid.)

Chapter 12: World's Parliament of Religions

123 (Daniel Dorchester, *History of Christianity*, Nabu Press, 1888, 2010 revision, 742.)

124 ("Voices from the World's Parliament of Religions, 1983," Boston Collaborative Encyclopedia of Western Theology, accessed June 25, 2019, https://tinyurl.com/y4ohbk2b.)

125 (Michael J. Altman, *Heathen, Hindoo, Hindu*, Oxford University Press, 2017.)

126 ("Parliament of the World's Religions 1893," Parliament of the World's Religions, accessed Febuary 27, 2019, https://tinyurl.com/y6fdw9a4.)

127 (Parliament, Soyen, ibid.)

128 (Parliament, Eastman, ibid.)

129 (Parliament, Silverman, ibid.)

130 (Parliament, Vivekananda, ibid.)

131 ("John Henry Barrows," Revolvy, accessed July 2, 2017, https://www.revolvy.com/topic/John%20Henry%20Barrows.)

132 (Walter R. Houghton, ed., "World's Parliament of Religions," *Neely's History of the Partliament of Religions and Religious Congresses*, Vol. 1, F.T. Neely, 1893, 34.)

133 (Marcus, Braybrooke, *Interfaith Organizations 1893-1979: An Historical Dictionary*, Edwin Mello Press, 1980, 8.)

134 (John H. Barrows, *The World's Parliament of Religions*, Parliament Publishing Co., 1893, 1572.)

135 (Voices, 214.)

Chapter 13: One Nation, Under God

136 (Jon Butler, Grant Wacker and Randall Balmer, Religion in America: A Short History, Oxford University Press, 2011, chap. 8, Apple E-book.)

137 (Ibid.)

138 (Donald M. Scott, "Divining America: Religion in American History — The Religious Origins of Manifest Destiny," Teacherserve, 2013, https://tinyurl.com/y3chhb4p.)

139 ("History of 'In God We Trust,'" U.S. Department of Treasury, last updated 2011, https://tinyurl.com/88t8ln9.)

140 (Maureen Malone, "Why Doesn't Every President Use the Lincoln Bible?" *Slate*, January 29, 2009, https://tinyurl.com/y2pxr9qw.)

141 ("Obama Using Two Bibles at Swearing-In Ceremony," *VOA News*, 2013, https://tinyurl.com/y5f6u9z6.)

142 (Linda Howard, "The Politicization of Science Education," IFS101@ SMCC, accessed January 15, 2015, https://tinyurl.com/y5w4p8lq.)

143 (Thomas T. McAvoy, "The Catholic Minority after the Americanist Controversy, 1899-1917: A Survey," JSTOR, 1959, Vol. 21, No. 1, http://www.jstor.org/stable/1405340?seq=1#page_scan_tab_contents.)

144 ("The Global Catholic Population," Pew Research Center, last updated February 13, 2013, http://www.pewforum.org/2013/02/13/the-global-catholic-population/.)

145 ("America's Changing Religious Landscape," Pew Research Center: Religion in American Life, last updated May 12, 2015, https://tinyurl.com/ldnxabw.)

146 (Sarah Pulliam Bailey, "Christianity Faces Sharp Decline as Americans are Becoming Even Less Affiliated with Religion," *The Washington Post*, May 12, 2015, https://tinyurl.com/zpns2j2.)

147 (Niall McCarthy, "Western Europe's Religiously Unaffiliated," Statistica, last updated June 5, 2018, https://tinyurl.com/y6ezj4sx.)

148 (Ibid.)

149 ("Global Christianity: A Report on the Size and Distribution of the World's Christian Population," Pew Research Center, last updated December 2011, https://tinyurl.com/nx4eoq7.)

150 (Melani McAlister, *The Kingdom of God has No Borders: A Global History*, Oxford University Press, 2018, https://tinyurl.com/yyqlzmgh.)

151 ("U.S. Public Becoming Less Religious," Pew Research Center, last updated 2015, https://tinyurl.com/y4566xlf.)

152 (David Masci, "Christianity Poised to Continue Its Shift from Europe to Africa," Pew Research Center, last updated April 7, 2015, https://tinyurl.com/y6gvw8ee.)

153 ("Worlds Apart: Religion in Canada, Britain, U.S.," Gallop, last updated Augst 12, 2003, https://tinyurl.com/yc3pxsw.)

154 (Naftali Bendavid, "Europe's Churches Go On Sale," *The Wall Street Journal*, January 5, 2015. https://tinyurl.com/y6ts5a74.)

155 ("America's Changing Religious Landscape," Pew Research Center, last updated May 12, 2015, https://tinyurl.com/ldnxabw.)

156 (Warren J. Blumenfeld, "Christian Privilege and Mainline Christianity in Public Schooling and in the Larger Society," *Equity and Excellence in Education*, Vol. 3, issue 3, 195-210, https://tinyurl.com/y57xf5oy.)

157 (Schlosser, "Christian Privilege," 31.1, 44-51.)

158 (Antonin Scalia, "God's Justice and Ours," First Things, last updated May 2015, 17-21, http://www.firstthings.com/ftissues/ft0205/.)

159 (Ruth Marcus, "What the Supreme Court Got Wrong on Prayer," *The Washington Post*, May 7, 2014, https://tinyurl.com/nlhtweq.)

160 (Ibid.)

161 (Richard Cohen, "The Supreme Court is Wrong: Prayers Divide," The Washington Post, May 6, 2014, https://tinyurl.com/y6gb4oj9.)

162 (Brett Martel, "Storms Payback from God, Naglin Says," *The Washington Post*, January 17, 2006, https://tinyurl.com/brx5w.)

163 ("Franklin: 'I Would Never Say This is God's Judgment," CNN, October 4, 2005, http://www.cnn.com/2005/US/10/04/cnna.graham/.)

Chapter 14: Monkey Trial Redux

164 (Matthew Chapman, *40 Days and 40 Nights*, Harper Collins, 2007, pt. 1, chap. 1, Apple E-book.)

165 (Adrian J. Desmond, "Charles Darwin, British Naturalist," Britannica.com, last updated March 8, 2019, https://www.britannica.com/biography/Charles-Darwin.)

166 (Katherine Stewart, "What 'Government Schools' Critics Really Mean," The New York Times, July 31, 2017, https://tinyurl.com/y3omqe2u.)

167 (Sean Scully, "'Breathtaking Inanity': How Intelligent Design Flunked its Test Case," Time, December 20, 2005, http://content.time.com/time/health/article/0,8599,1142625-1,00.html.)

168 (Ibid.)

169 (Ibid.)

170 (Ibid.)

171 (Katherine Stewart, *The Good News Club: The Religious Right's Stealth Assault on America's Children*, PublicAffairs, 2012, 7.)

Chapter 15: Christian Identity

172 (Liam Stack, "A Brief History of Deadly Attacks on Abortion Providers," *The New York Times*, November 29, 2015, https://tinyurl.com/y85nn9kn.)

173 (Ebra Kelly, "10 Doomsday Cults of the 20th Century," *Listverse*, October 19, 2016, http://listverse.com/2016/10/19/10-doomsday-cults-of-the-20th-century/.)

Chapter 16: Speaking in Tongues

174 ("Pentecostal Resource Page," Pew Research Center, last updated October 5, 2006, http://www.pewforum.org/2006/10/05/pentecostal-resource-page/.)

175 (Ibid.)

176 (John Gordon Melton, "Pentecostalism," Britannica,com, last updated August 31, 2014, http://www.britannica.com/EBchecked/topic/450414/Pentecostalism.)

177 (Haak and Vijgen, "Atlas of Pentecostalism.")

178 (Melton, Ibid.)

179 (David Filipov, "Why More Than a Million Russians Have Lined Up to See a Piece of the Rib of Saint Nicholas," *The Washington Post*, June 29, 2017, https://tinyurl.com/y39t5rmq.)

Chapter 17: Missing Hotel Bibles

180 (Roya Wolverson, "The Hotel Room Bible on the Outs," *Newsweek*, November 7, 2007, https://www.newsweek.com/hotel-room-bible-outs-96885.)

181 (Hugo Martin, "More Hotels are Checking Out of the Bible Business," *Los Angeles Times*, December 4, 2016, http://www.latimes.com/business/la-fi-hotel-bibles-20161204-story.html.)

Chapter 18: Resurrecting Socrates

182 (Douglas N. Morgan and Charner Perry, "The Teaching of Philosophy in American Schools," American Psychological Association journal, 1958-59, vol. 32, 91-137, http://www.jstor.org/stable/3129324.)

183 (N.A. Calkins, "Report of the Committee of Ten on Secondary School Studies," National Education Association, 1894, https://tinyurl.com/y4uev442.)

184 (Ibid.)

185 (Ibid.)

186 (Anaïs Chartschenko, "My Meaningless Diploma," *Leaving Fundamentalism* blog, Patheos, November 25, 2013, https://tinyurl.com/y3dpege4)

187 (Anaïs Chartschenko, "My First Time With Shakespeare," *Leaving Fundamentalism* blog, Patheos, June 14, 2017, https://tinyurl.com/yxobknya.)

188 (Tara Westover, *Educated*. Random House, 2018.)

189 (Stephan Millett and Alan Tapper, "Benefits of Collaborative Philosophical Inquiry in Schools," *Educational Philosophy and Theory*, 2012, vol. 44, issue 5, https://tinyurl.com/y38r3xyf.)

190 (W. Richard Walker, Steven J. Hoekstra and Rodney J. Vogl, "Science Education No Guarantee of Skepticism," *Skeptic*, 2002, vol. 9, issue 3, 24-25.)

A Proposal

191 (Christopher Hitchins, *The Portable Atheist: Essential Readings for the Nonbeliever*, Da Capo Press, 2007, intro., Apple E-book.)

192 (Ibid., ch. 1.)

193 (Ibid., intro.)

194 (Ibid., ch. 1.)

195 ("Younger People are Less Religious Than Older Ones in Many Countries, Especially in the U.,S. and Europe," Pew Research Center, last updated June 13, 2018.)

196 (David Leonhardt, "The Rise of Young Americans Who Don't Believe in God," *The New York Times*, May 12, 2015, https://tinyurl.com/y6tn92um.)

197 (Pew, "Younger People.")

198 (David Masci, "Q&A: Why Millennials are less religious than older Americans," Pew Research Center, last updated January 8, 2016, https://tinyurl.com/j84sh8h.)

199 (Robert A. Hinde, *Why Gods Persist: A Scientific Approach to Religion*, Routledge, 1999, ch. 17, Apple E-book.)

200 (Chris Mooney, "The Science of Whyi We Don't Believe in Science," *Mother Jones*, May/June 2011, https://tinyurl.com/y3evrud3.)

201 (Robert Todd Carroll, "Motivated Reasoning," The Skeptics Dictionary, 2016, http://www.skepdic.com/motivatedreasoning.html.)

202 (Daniel W. Drezner, "Why Free Speech on Campus is Not as Simple as Everyone Thinks," *The New York Times*, March 23, 2015, https://tinyurl.com/yxmu56ec.)

203 (Michael Shammas, "For a Better Society, Teach Philosophy in High Schools," *The Huffington Post*, February 25, 2016, https://tinyurl.com/y5wg2j5a.)

204 (Victor J. Stenger, *God: The Failed Hypothesis — How Science Shows That God Does Not Exist*, Prometheus Books, 2007, chap. 9, Apple eBook.)

205 (Richard Dawkins, *The God Delusion*, 2006, Houghton Mifflin, chap. 3, Apple E-book.)

206 (Ibid.)

207 (Ibid.)

208 (Ibid., ch. 4.)

209 (Dean Hamer, *The God Gene: How Faith is Hardwired into our Genes*, Doubleday, 2004, chap. 11, Apple E-book.)

210 (Wheen, introduction.)

211 (Jesse Bering, *The Belief Instinct: The Psychology of Souls, Destiny and the Meaning of Life*, W.W. Norton & Co., 2011, epigraph, Apple E-book.)

212 (Mark Murphy, "What did Marx Mean by Thesis Eleven?" *Social Theory Applied*, last updated August 10, 2016, https://tinyurl.com/y66z8djj.)

213 ("U.S. Religious Landscape Survey," Pewforum.org, 2019, https://www.pewforum.org/religious-landscape-study/)

Made in the USA
Middletown, DE
15 December 2020